Resolute

Geo Dunn Dfc Ld'H

10 76608 149 Mel Flt

RESOLUTE

To war with
Bomber
Command
George Dunn
DFC, Ld'H *and*
Ferris Newton
DFM
with Steve Darlow

Published in 2020 by Fighting High Ltd,
www.fightinghigh.com

Copyright © Fighting High Ltd, 2020
Copyright text © Steve Darlow, 2020
Copyright text © George Dunn, 2020
Copyright text © Ferris Newton, 2020

The rights of Ferris Newton, George Dunn and Steve Darlow
to be identified as the author of this book are asserted in
accordance with the Copyright, Patents and Designs Act 1988.

British Library Cataloguing-in-Publication data. A CIP
record for this title is available from the British Library.

ISBN – 13-978-0-9934152-0-3

Designed and typeset in Adobe Minion 11/15pt
by Michael Lindley (www.truthstudio.co.uk.)

Printed and bound in Wales by Gomer Press.
Front cover design by Truthstudio Limited

To our rear gunner Cyril Dean, affectionately known as Dixie.

Contents

Foreword

by Officer Commanding Battle of Britain Memorial Flight,
Squadron Leader Mark 'Disco' Discombe AFC

The sheer bravery of the aircrew that served in Bomber Command during the Second World War is staggering. The chances of surviving two operational tours amounting to 50 operations, which usually qualified aircrew to be relieved from the front line, was woefully low. However, many tens of thousands of ordinary men volunteered to fly on ops, and help put a stop to the encroaching evil of Nazi Germany.

The RAF Battle of Britain Memorial Flight's Lancaster is kept airworthy as a memorial to those men and the 55,573 that paid the ultimate sacrifice. (Recent research by the International Bomber Command Centre reveals that this immediate post-war official number is probably exceeded by many more.) No other aircraft in the Flight's hangar at RAF Coningsby represents such a loss of life, yet fortitude in the face of overwhelming danger. The most common words heard when we have the privilege to talk to Bomber Command veterans are 'I was only doing my job', signifying how humble the George and Ferris' of the world are. The stories I have heard, told in an unassuming and matter of fact tone, are what films have been made of.

The honour of listening to these stories is not lost on any member of the Flight and remains the best part of the job. It was these ordinary heroes that turned the aircraft of Bomber Command into war winners; ordinary young men like George and Ferris.

October 2020

Introduction

I met George Dunn about ten years ago during the campaign to raise funds for the Bomber Command Memorial. He was part of the remarkable Bomber Command Aircrew Veterans Group Sussex that had formed to help with the fundraising. What an extraordinary group of veterans, brilliantly and conscientiously chaperoned by Cherry Greveson. Sadly, so many are no longer with us, but they achieved their objective. Not only the building of the memorial but a considerable rise in the public awareness of what they and their colleagues experienced and achieved.

I instantly took a liking to George, as have my wife and sons; indeed, as has anyone who meets him. He is a charmer with an infectious laugh and smile. He is also humble, but willing to share his time. George has become a firm favourite at book signings and events across the country, and I am honoured to call him a friend. (Hopefully he reciprocates.)

Over the years George has helped me with other books relating to Bomber Command, but it soon became apparent that George merited a book of his own. However, he was reluctant. He claimed he did not have a story. At many book signings people were asking George when he would be writing his book. 'Oh, others did more than me', was the usual response. I am sure that many readers of this book, having read his story, will, like me, beg to differ. It is a story certainly worth telling.

Finally, in 2019, we persuaded George to start work on his book. George's memory is sharp and he has vivid recollections of his wartime days. In addition his flight engineer, Ferris Newton, who sadly died at the age of seventy-four, had written his story many years before, and we made contact with Ferris's stepdaughter, Caroline Bolton, who kindly gave us permission to work with Ferris's account, and make this a jointly authored book. (We all agreed that the royalties from the book would go to the Royal Air Force Benevolent Fund who are the guardians of the Bomber Command Memorial in The Green Park, London.) Bomb-aimer Andrew Maitland, who flew his first tour with George, and went on to a second tour as a Pathfinder, had also published his story, *Through the Bombsight*, so there was plenty of first-hand material to draw upon.

For context in the book I have relied upon the 'bible' for those researching Bomber Command, *The Bomber Command War Diaries* by Martin Middlebrook and Chris Everitt, and the superb and vital *Bomber Command Losses* series of books written by Bill Chorley. Indeed, Bill also wrote *To See The Dawn Breaking – 76 Squadron Operations*. George and Ferris's first tour was with No. 76 Squadron. The title of this book is *Resolute*, which is the No. 76 Squadron motto. George will not like me saying this but that word epitomises what he did in 1943. George flew his first tour, with Ferris, during one of the most intense periods of the air war: the Battle of the Ruhr, the Battle of Hamburg, the Peenemünde raid and the initial raids of the winter offensive of late 1943. The attrition rates were high. So many of George's friends and colleagues were lost. Enough to test the resolve of any man. Despite the odds, despite the risks and danger, George and Ferris remained resolute.

Steve Darlow
September 2020

Chapter One

Keen

George was keen to do his bit.

When war broke out with Germany on 3 September 1939, George Dunn, from Whitstable on the north Kent coast, was approaching his seventeenth birthday, but it would be some months before he had the opportunity to take up arms, of sorts. The period known as the Phoney War followed, with only limited action in western Europe.In April 1940, however, German troops invaded Denmark and Norway. The following month the Wehrmacht forced its way into the Netherlands, Belgium and Holland. All three countries eventually capitulated, and the British Expeditionary Force was forced into a mass evacuation of troops from the beaches around Dunkirk. The English Channel was all that separated Britain from the Nazi aggression. The fear of an invasion increased, whether seaborne or from the air, and calls for some kind of a home defence force grew. A few days after the German Blitzkrieg opened on the low countries, Secretary of State for War Anthony Eden broadcast the formation of the Local Defence Volunteers (which would become the 'Home Guard'), with the promise of uniforms and weapons. George's opportunity had arrived. 'A queue formed at the local police station in order to register and subsequently we were directed to the local drill hall, normally used by the Territorial Army.' The initial issue of kit fell short of Anthony Eden's initial promise; 'All we had was an armband with LDV on, no weapons.'

> In some ways I suppose it seemed a bit of a laugh as at that time we did not have any weapons, but we all took it seriously, especially as we had no idea how the war would develop. There was talk of German parachutists dropping from the sky over Britain and we would be expected to defend such places as gas works, water works, and roadblocks.
>
> As time went on we received uniforms to replace the LDV armband and also received a supply of Lee Enfield .303 rifles and bayonets, plus a Vickers machine gun. Weapons training and drill was given and we were formed into platoons so that eventually we began to look more like an army capable of putting up some sort of resistance should an invasion take place.

Two pictures exist of George during his time with the LDV/Home Guard. A youthful exuberance is clear on the faces of George and those with him: John Castle, who went on to serve as groundcrew with the RAF; 'Chummy' Nutten, who served in the Navy and was taken prisoner by the Japanese; Roy Olive, who lost his life flying as navigator in a No. 77 Squadron Halifax on the raid to Nuremberg on the night of 27/28 August 1943.

> I had an enjoyable time serving in this capacity and even learned to drive an old van that we used as the company transport. Our night duties took us to various places in the district, but the one we most enjoyed was being on duty at Headquarters where there were cooking facilities. We had a butcher in our platoon and we often had a lovely meal of bangers and mash.
>
> I was usually doing Home Guard duties three nights a

week and fire watching at night for Pickford's Removals, my
daytime employers. So most weeks I was on some sort of duty
for five or six nights, which at times proved quite tiring. By
August 1940 the Battle of Britain was in full swing and many
dogfights took place over Kent. Being young I thought, God
I wouldn't mind being up there myself. We were always on
the lookout for any German pilots who had bailed out of
their aircraft.

During the summer of 1940, with the Luftwaffe attempting to
destroy the Royal Air Force in preparation for an invasion, George,
from his home town of Whitstable, could watch the combats and
the contrails, 'and when the London Blitz started the German
bombers, hordes of them, came up the Thames Estuary'. From
September 1940 through to May the following year the Luftwaffe
Blitz, the bombing of towns and cities across the country, would
kill tens of thousands of civilians. An assault described by the future
Commander-in-Chief of Bomber Command, Sir Arthur Harris,
as 'sowing the wind'.

Early in 1941 George decided not to wait for his call-up papers: 'I
didn't fancy the Army, and I had a fear of water – I didn't fancy
drowning. So I thought I would get in before my call-up.'

I went to the RAF recruiting office at Chatham to volunteer
for aircrew training as a wireless operator/air gunner. After
an educational test and medical I went before a selection
board of three officers and was subsequently asked if I would
consider training as a pilot, which rather took me by surprise.
I thought that my educational qualifications were not high
enough. However I was happy to accept their judgement.
    They stamped my national identity card with 'u/t pilot',
under training pilot, and eventually I went to Uxbridge and
took the King's shilling.

It was June 1941 before I received my call-up and I proceeded to an RAF receiving centre at Babbacombe, near Torquay, staying at the Sefton Hotel. We were kitted out with uniforms and received basic drill and instruction on RAF law.

A week later George was transferred to No. 8 Initial Training Wing, Newquay, and a six-week course, including basic mathematics, elementary navigation, Air Force law, aircraft recognition, 'and plenty of drill, swimming and cross-country runs. Having always been a keen sportsman the physical side of the course came easier to me than some of the others.' Passing his end of course examination resulted in a promotion to Leading Aircraftman and the wearing of the white flash in George's forage cap, recognising he was aircrew under training.

Following some leave George was sent to West Kirby, near Liverpool, a transit centre for overseas drafts. 'Unfortunately after a few weeks there I was taken ill with appendicitis and peritonitis. It was a very near do and they sent for my parents to come up from Whitstable because they thought I might be a gonner. I spent three weeks in hospital plus a spell of sick leave.' George's flying aspirations were now in doubt and he had to attend a medical board at RAF Halton to assess his fitness. 'To my dismay I was graded for UK duties only for six months. As there was very little elementary flying in this country, I could see my flying career being put back for some considerable time.'

However, I still had to return to West Kirby and much to my surprise I was put on a draft for Southern Rhodesia. I was in two minds as to whether to accept it or not. Having always had a preference for Canada, so I saw the warrant officer at the end of parade, said they would have to take me off draft, and produced my Home Service grading document. After several more weeks, kicking my heels, I was sent to Heaton Park, Manchester, another transit camp, and billeted with a young couple with whom I still exchange Christmas cards to this day. Life in the camp was pretty boring as there were no facilities except for training and apart from drill, most of our time was spent on general duties such as weeding and other sorts of fatigues. A poor way of going on really!

As Christmas 1941 approached, George recalls the 'magic day' when he found himself on draft again, 'and this time for Canada'.

So I kept very quiet about my UK-only grading and kept my fingers crossed right until I was aboard ship. On 23 December 1941 we set sail for Halifax, Nova Scotia, on a terrible Norwegian liner called the *SS Bergensfjord* that was being used as a troop ship. It was difficult to find a place to sling a hammock due to the crowded conditions and I finished up finding a spot in a hammock rack. Owing to the rough weather conditions at that time of the year it was not very long before the majority of the draft were very badly seasick and bodies were lying prostrate everywhere, with a sickening smell wherever one went. My bout lasted for 36 hours and I almost wished for a U-boat to come along and put us out of our misery.

After a few days things became somewhat better and we were able to partake of the not particularly good food provided on board. It was a relief to arrive at Halifax and we were put straight on a train.

George arrived at the transit camp at Moncton. Life was looking up. 'Our meal that night was a sight to behold: eggs, bacon, sausages, and chips, with lashings of bread, jam, cream, orange juice, cakes and so on – things which we had not seen on our dining tables for a very long time. We thought this is going to be great. Nine months of this and we are really going to enjoy it.' George was soon placed on draft for Caron, eighteen miles from Moose Jaw, Saskatchewan. 'The train journey took three days and we were sitting on slatted

wooden seats, so our rear ends were well and truly marked by the
time we reached our destination. And so began elementary flying
training on Tiger Moths.'

In September 1940, at the height of the Battle of Britain, British Prime
Minister Winston Churchill proclaimed, 'The fighters are our
salvation, but the bombers alone provide the means of victory.' But
it was clear, at that stage, that Bomber Command was far from
being an effective potential contributor to final victory. High loss
rates on daylight raids in the early stages of the war, and during the
Battle of France, made it clear that Bomber Command, in terms
of men, materiel and strategy, fell short of the 'means' required. A
rapid expansion was initiated in terms of airfield construction,
aircraft design and manufacture, alongside the recruitment and
training of personnel. The hostile skies above Britain were no place
for fledgling aircrew to find their wings. That would have to be
achieved overseas, and tens of thousands of recruits, like George,
were to become part of the remarkable British Commonwealth Air
Training Plan. In December 1939 an agreement between the United
Kingdom, Canada, Australia and New Zealand opened the way for
tens of thousands of trainee aircrew to learn their trade at schools
across the dominions teaching elementary flying training, air
navigation, bombing, gunnery and wireless skills. On 5 January
1942 No. 33 Elementary Flying Training School opened at Caron,
Saskatchewan, Canada. As George Dunn recalled, 'Caron itself
consisted of two grain elevators, a few dwellings, and the airfield. As
the snow was very thick at the time it really did look very desolate.'

Our quarters were quite comfortable and well heated despite
the extreme cold, but any illusions we had about partaking of
some very good food were quickly dispelled as we found out
that we were on RAF rations and not RCAF rations. So even
though we were in Canada where all types of food were still
plentiful, we were no better off than those back in the UK.

KEEN   7

Consequently, we spent a lot of our time and what little cash we had consuming bacon and eggs and ice cream at Smoky Joe's wooden shack of a café just outside the main gates.

The snow was quite heavy and was not expected to clear before the end of April, so for the whole of the time we were due to spend there we knew it would be very cold and that identifying landmarks would not be easy. Half a day was spent on flying and the other half on ground instruction covering theory of flight, engines, airframes, navigation and so on.

George took to the air on 11 January 1942, his first ever flight. 'Due to the impatience of my instructor I did not perform at all well during the first few days. At one stage I thought I would never make it. He was one of those chaps that would snatch the stick out of your hand. As it was, if you weren't doing very well, they gave you another instructor. This time I got an ex-Battle of Britain pilot, Flying Officer Boot. He was a different cup of tea altogether. We got on straight away, no problems.' (The only pilot with the surname 'Boot' listed as having taken part in the Battle of Britain is Peter Boot, who served with No. 1 Squadron flying Hurricanes during the Battle of France and Battle of Britain, and was credited with six confirmed victories and one damaged.)

The change of instructor was indeed well received and after a check from the flight commander George went solo, 'it felt marvellous'. A test flight with the chief flying instructor followed and then a solo cross-country flight, with only a map as a navigation aid. By the end of the course, graded as 'Average', George had recoded 32.45 hours of dual and 30.15 hours as pilot. On 12 March it was time for George to move on to the next stage of his training at No. 41 Service Flying Training School (SFTS) at Weyburn, south-east of Moose Jaw, flying Avro Ansons. 'I had my first flight on 9 April and went solo on 4 May after about 10 hours of instruction.'

About halfway through the course I was called to the medical

officer. He said to me, 'What are you doing out here?' I played
dumb. 'Don't know what you mean sir.' He said, 'You're on
Home Service only, you should never have been put on draft.'
I replied, 'Well you always carry out orders.' He looked at me
rather quizzically. I had to undergo a full medical, including
a decompression chamber test up in Regina. Fortunately
I passed.

The flying side of the course at SFTS was more intensive
and involved a lot more cross-country flights. We finally
finished the course on 28 July and were awarded our wings.
It was quite a day for celebration, which concluded with a
night out with the instructors. By this time, I had amassed
a total of 213 hours' flying time.

George began the journey home, which included a visit to Toronto
to call on relatives. In August it was time to run the gauntlet of the
Atlantic, eventually arriving in Greenock, Scotland. A posting to
Bournemouth followed, 'where it was a question of hanging around
waiting for a posting to an RAF station. Fortunately this came very
quickly. Most wanted to be on fighters. We were asked for our
preference, and the majority of people said fighters, but at that time
Bomber Command was being built up and they were short of pilots.
Nearly everybody was allocated to Bomber Command. Knowing
that all the other people were in the same boat, you accepted it.'

Arriving at No. 6 Advanced Flying Unit, RAF Chipping Norton,
Oxfordshire, George started to put in the hours on Airspeed
Oxfords. 'Very similar to an Anson except they were slightly more
difficult to fly. I commenced flying on 24 September 1942 and things
soon came back despite not having flown for two months. I went
solo three days later. It was now a question of getting used to flying
in this country, especially at night where our black-out regulations
contrasted greatly with the lit-up areas in Canada.' Finishing in the
middle of October George spent a week at RAF Honington, Suffolk,
on a standard beam approach course, 'designed to enable one to

know how to locate a beam whilst on instruments, and be able to land in low cloud and poor visibility using the beam'. With 261 hours' flying time to his name, a journey north followed, to No. 20 Operational Training Unit at RAF Lossiemouth, Scotland, and 'meeting up with navigators, air gunners, and others to form a crew – this was left entirely to the airmen themselves. In a short time friendships were made and crews were formed. The first chap I met was Andy Maitland, from Ayr, Scotland, a bomb-aimer, and he said to me, "Are you crewed up yet?" I said, "No", to which he replied, "Well I'm looking for a pilot, can we get together?" "Yes".

After the war Andy Maitland would write his own account of his war years in his book *Through the Bombsight*, which included meeting his first crew:

Our first priority on starting the OTU course was to sort ourselves into crews and this was most important as we would stay with our selected crews for the remainder of our training and for our first tour of operations against the enemy. One can well understand it was very necessary to crew with men who as far as possible had similar interests and were likely to work well together with the minimum friction or argument and who would in the end make an efficient operational bomber crew.

About this time I had met George Dunn, a sergeant pilot, about the same age as myself. We were both very keen on sport and often played football together. We appeared to have a good rapport going between us so it was decided we should crew together.

[George:] Andy said, 'By the way I've met an Irish navigator, he's a pilot officer, and he's looking to be crewed up so shall I have a word with him?' 'Yes, sure.' Reg McCadden from Belfast joined us as navigator.

[Andy Maitland:] Reginald McCadden, a flying officer

navigator, was a Belfast man about 27 years of age and
married. He had been involved in local government and
was studying for an economics degree before coming into
the Service. Like George and myself he was very keen on sport
and all three of us seemed to be on the same wavelength.

Sergeant Jock Todd was about 28 years of age and hailed
from Montrose. He was married with a keen sense of humour
and was also keen on sport; he was to fit into our crew as the
wireless operator. Jock often would say to me, 'Let's not spend
too much time in the target area. I am too young to die.'

Sergeant Dixie Dean, a young Canadian from Toronto, was
to be our rear gunner. He was only about 19 years of age and
was full of life. His favourite saying when things were not
going right for him was, 'You goddam son of a bitch.' A very
headstrong young man with his own ideas on how to live life
to the full.

[George:] A sixth member would join us later at Heavy
Conversion unit. 'Joe' Scrivener, an ex-physical training
instructor in the RAF who had remustered to aircrew, would
join us as an air gunner. Joe hailed from King's Cross in
London and was quite a character with 'wide boy'
characteristics. It was amazing the strings he seemed to be
able to pull when necessary, to the benefit of us all.

[Andy Maitland:] Joe was a bundle of fun and one seldom
found him without a smile on his face. He was from London,
married, and was a few years older than Reg. Before the RAF
he had been involved in a good retailing business and used to
tell us he had many contacts in the City of London and he
could always find someone to supply goods that were in short
supply. His cheery chatter always kept us amused and he
could always be relied on to come up with a funny story when
least expected.

[George:] A flight engineer, Ferris Newton, would also join us at the conversion unit. Meanwhile, our current crew of five spent a couple of weeks at Lossiemouth on classroom instruction and general drill plus some fatigues.

For the first half of January 1943 George gained experience as a second pilot on the Vickers Wellington. On 28 January, as first pilot flying his crew and two other airmen, he recorded a four-hour flight in his logbook, 'X Country Bombing – Sim Bombing Air to Sea Firing Photography'. Through February and into early March there were further cross-countries at night as well as bombing practice and air firing. George was certainly starting to feel confident with his crew:

We gelled straight away. I instilled in them right from the start that it's got to be teamwork. No individuals. If we were going to get through it had got to be teamwork. Eventually when we got to a squadron, we used to go out to dispersal and the crew would swap jobs. I'd get somebody to go onto the radio, so that they could send out an SOS. The wireless operator was already a gunner. Andy, the bomb-aimer, was fairly good at navigation anyway, so he could take over if the navigator got killed or injured. We came together very well and in an emergency we could have coped.

A lot of the flying was done at night and included several cross-country flights, some photography and practice bombing with small practice bombs plus one flight with a 500lb bomb to be dropped on a target out at sea. This flight, as far as we were concerned, was quite eventful as the bombing mechanism failed to operate and it was only by violent manoeuvring that I was able to shake off the bomb before returning to base. We then had to hand-wind the under carriage down as the hydraulics had failed and then land without flaps, which involved a much flatter and faster

approach to the landing strip. All my flying up to now had
been carried out on grass airfields and the flare paths
consisted of goose neck paraffin flares.

Reg McCadden had a lucky escape during one training flight, as
George recalls. 'They would put two or three navigators together
with a crew to do night flight navigation. They lost an engine one
night and they had to bail out. He got away with it, but broke his
little finger.'
Unfortunately many aircrew under training did not get away
with it. One of the most shocking casualty statistics associated with
Bomber Command is that around 8,000 lives were lost in training
accidents. George's first flight at No. 20 OTU Lossiemouth was on
2 January 1943, and his last two months later on 4 March, a period
in which he spent just short of 100 hours in the air on Wellingtons.
In that period William Chorley's Bomber Command losses book
covering OTU training fatalities records the following loss statistics
in regard to No. 20 OTU:

5 January 1943.	Wellington 1C R3232 –	six lives lost.
10 January 1943.	Wellington 1C T2713 –	one life lost.
19 January 1943.	Wellington 1C HD985 –	six lives lost.
24 January 1943.	Wellington 1C N2769 –	five lives lost.
28 January 1943.	Wellington 1C HF858 –	five lives lost.
28 February 1943.	Wellington 1C N2823 –	three lives lost.

Twenty-six trained airmen killed, owing to crashes from engine
failures or lost over the sea. Luck held no respect for experience or
rank, those dying ranging from sergeants to a squadron leader.
Having completed their initial crew training it was time to
transfer to a heavy conversion unit to gain experience on flying a
four-engined heavy bomber, to pick up another gunner, Joe
Scrivener, and a flight engineer, Ferris Newton.

Chapter Two

Flight Mechanic to Flight Engineer

Royal Air Force new recruit Ferris Newton noted in his diary the first mistake he made in the Air Force: 'Joined the longest queue I had ever seen for tea. Cheese Pie. Did not like it then and still don't.' A second mistake soon followed: 'Put a spoonful of salt in my tea thinking it was sugar. Too scared to go and get some more tea.'

Earlier in the day Ferris had left Leeds by train, destined for Padgate, 'a large recruiting and training depot near Warrington. After filling in bags of forms and answering numerous questions, given a slip of paper with my number 1018086 rank AC2, u/t FMA, and name.' Ferris received his 'Mug, knife, fork, and spoon', and then 'Bed, three biscuits, and four blankets'. Then it was time for tea and his encounter with the Cheese Pie.

In the evening, thought I would try the NAAFI [Navy, Army and Air Force Institutes] for a supper. There was an even longer queue than at tea. Gave it up, found a corner, sat down and wrote my first letter home. Felt very miserable. Ended up spending the night in the air raid shelter. A raid on Liverpool.

The following day, 30 August 1940, Ferris was issued with the rest of his equipment, 'blue, boots, webbing etc. Not allowed to put on our blue as we were moving the next day. Another night spent in the air raid shelter, had an alert in the afternoon as well.' On the final day of the month Ferris found himself as one of 'another hundred recruits', sent to West Kirby.

> Here for about three weeks. This is the place where you go in a rookie and come out an Airman (they hope). Square bashing, saluting to the left and right, rifle drill and firing, P.T., health, sex, gas lectures, and not forgetting the good old jabs, the M.O.'s favourite pastime. On the third week when we were allowed out Catherine came over to see her 'Airman husband'. Got a bit of a shock as I had to wear a 'cheese cutter' about a couple of sizes too big for us. Cath had a bad time, poor hotel and air raids. Glad to get back home.

On 24 September 1940 Ferris was posted to RAF Hednesford and No. 6 School of Technical Training, to begin mechanical training on airframes and engines. 'First impression of Hednesford. Complete isolation. Camp stuck on top of big hill known as kit bag hill. High pressure "bull". Hadn't been in the place for ten minutes when a Cpl. [Corporal] told us all to clean the back of our cap badges as well as the front.'

Ferris was similarly not enamoured with the flight sergeant in command of his wing, who introduced himself, 'I'm known here as Billie the Bastard and I live up to my name.' Two weeks of general duties followed, and incentives were offered to those who had the cleanest hut, given 'the honour of flying the C.O. flag'. If the flag was held for four weeks, each member of that hut received a free ticket to the camp cinema and voucher for the NAAFI. Ferris recorded, 'Hut 29 was never in the running. Made one or two pals by this time. Joe from Leeds, Charlie from Bradford, Jack from Wigan, Bob and Jock from Bonnie Scotland. 28 men all told in the hut and all of them a pretty decent bunch.'

Over the next seventeen weeks Ferris underwent basic training and various courses including rigging, splicing, fabric, hydraulics, carpentry, metal repairs, and maintenance and inspection. On 29 January Ferris wrote in his diary, 'I'm now Flt/Mec. A.C.2. Newton. Some rank?'

Felt rather pleased with myself, managed to have passed the course without previous knowledge of aeroplanes. Got a rank although it's the bottom, no more u/t [under training] before my name at any rate. Sent home on fourteen days leave with full kit. Posting instructions will be sent to my home. So it was with much pleasure that I said farewell to Hednesford, as I walked and half ran down 'kit bag' hill to the station.

Two weeks later Ferris's posting instructions arrived: No. 11 Operational Training Unit (OTU) RAF Bassingbourn. 'Never heard of the place,' was his response.

Get map out. Oh yes near Royston, about forty miles from London. Not too bad, could have been the Orkneys or someplace I suppose. Wonder if any of my pals will be there. Hope so. ... The aircraft were all Wellingtons. ... Worked pretty hard, bags of circuits and bumps knocked the stuffing out of the old Wimpys. Saw my first crash. Wimpy taking off on night flying, charging along the field when she burst a tyre, slewed round, went on her belly, and as she stopped burst into flames from nose to tail. Being fabric covered she was soon a blaze. None of the crew were saved.

In August 1941, Ferris, now an AC1, recorded, 'Camp bombed. One bomb landed on our block.'

Killed all but one chap in one room upstairs. He was lucky. Just happened to be at the toilets. Blast knocked poor Jack out of bed. Lucky for him the bomb fell at the other end. MY end. Lucky for me I was out on night flying.

Got a chance, through Jack, to come to Yorkshire. Dennis is going as well. All three of us came up in the car, getting the weekend at home, before proceeding to our new station. On the way up I was gonged by the police for going over 30 mph through Doncaster.

Three days later Ferris arrived at RAF Holme-on-Spalding-Moor, and No. 458 (RAAF) Squadron. 'Brand new squadrons, going to have Wellingtons when they arrive. Nothing organised at all.'

Didn't take the three of us long to find the quickest way to Leeds. Only forty miles away. After a week or so of running to Leeds and back things started to happen on the squadron. More men and NCOs, and even some kites. Operation to Leeds temporarily suspended. First operational kite A for Apple. Groundcrew of A Apple: Cpl. Tom Durrell, Fit. 2 E., AC1 Paddy Millam, FME, AC1 Ferris Newton, FMA, AC2 Bill Hutchinson, FMA. Flt/Sgt Banks i/c/ Flight, second in charge Sgt Lovelace.

Ferris managed to spend Christmas Day 1941 at home but had to return to Holme-on-Spalding-Moor, 'bright and early' on Boxing Day, 'as the squadron had to stand to'.

All the aircraft bombed up with armour piercing bombs and got ready. Rumour said it was to bomb Brest, but the aircraft never went. Plenty of snow about this time. The whole squadron called out to clear the main runway. First time I had seen rum issued.

Two aircraft burst out on dispersal on two successive nights. Everyone wondering whether it is sabotage, extra guard duties put on. A guard on every aircraft now. One

night Jack Dennis and myself were all on together, one of
the coldest nights of the winter. Jack was binding away from
going on at 1800 hours to coming off next morning. Why have
we to do guards? What's the RAF Regiment for? What are GDs
for? What about HQ staff etc. etc? Poor old Jack, he used to
hate guard duty. Well we all did.

On 3 March 1942 Ferris, now a LAC, wrote in his diary that he was
about to enjoy some embarkation leave. 'Medical inspection and
jabs. Felt a little rough after them. Half asleep on the first four days
of my seven.'

Went back from leave to the good news of overseas cancelled
for all English boys. All our places had been taken over by
Aussies. The aircrew flew their own kites out to the Middle
East. W/C Mulholland and crew shot down over the
Mediterranean on the way out. Rest of squadron now posted.
Jack went to Elsham in Lincs. Dennis and I went to Snaith.

On 28 March Ferris commented on his new home with No. 150
Squadron at RAF Snaith in Yorkshire.

Dennis and I were on No. 4 dispersal away down the road
for a couple of miles. Used to practise glider towing here. A
Halifax used to tow it about. The squadron actually operated
with Wellingtons, and as they had all been fitted with a new
secret radar aid (Gee box) we groundcrew types had to take
it in turns to sleep in the kites. Armed with a revolver we had
to climb in, close the trap door, and lay on it.

At Snaith Ferris did a 'Backers Up' course. 'It is now the fashion,
wherever you go, nearly one of the first jobs they give you is a
Backers Up course. This course is to enable you to assist the RAF
Regiment in the event of the aerodrome being attacked.'

The end of April 1942 found Ferris billeted in a requisitioned hotel in Bude, Cornwall, and attached to No. 1 AACU (Anti-Aircraft Co-operation Unit). His friend Dennis had been posted to a unit at Farnborough, 'so ended the story of three men and a car. The latter posted back into Civvy Street.'

The camp itself was a few miles out of Bude situated on the edge of the cliff at Cleave. Henley aircraft were used for the target towing, there were one or two Queen Bees, but they were not used very often. The Ack Ack guns were on the far side of the field firing out to sea. We had nice easy hours, no night flying. Of course we had guard duty to do, that's the curse of all Airmen except S.P.s, that's their job anyway. The Sgt. in charge of the S.P. was a bit of a stinker. Pulled me off parade one day for not having a haircut. Did I want to take his punishment, or should he put me on a charge? I accepted his punishment which was going down to the guard room and helping to clean it up, also help to feed the pigs.

The guard duties we had to do were on the main gate which involved plenty of saluting but not doing a hell of a lot of guarding. As if an intruder would come up to the main gate. No just another job to give the airmen, and it was a full 24 hour job. Those were the kind that used to get up your back, completely unnecessary. Another racket was a week on fire picket. Apart from one half day in the week when you sat on the fire tender the rest of the time was spent in anything but fires. Delivering coal, cookhouse fatigues, collecting the swill for the pigs etc. etc. We used to bind about it but it never did any good. I had some leave, 7 days plus a 48 hour pass for travelling which you needed. Took about 15 hours to get home, change at Oakhampton [sic], Exeter, and Bristol.

Bude is a very charming seaside town. Had a nice cinema and big hotels, quite a few of them being requisitioned by Government or Services. Used to go for some pleasant walks

on the cliff or inland to nearby villages. During the beginning
of June Mother came down to stay for a couple of weeks
holiday. I was posted the day before she was due to go back.
At home, Cath had been caught showing a light at the lounge
window.

On 11 June 1942 Ferris was posted on to a Fitter's course at RAF
Cosford. 'Usual effort the first two weeks. Backers Up training and
in between times gardening (this is a new one), cookhouse fatigues,
gas drills and all that. Put into No. 2 Wing with a Flt/Sgt Evans i/c
another Billie the Bastard type.' In July Ferris started on his fitter's
course: hydraulics, carpentry, metal repairs, corrosion of metals,
heat treatments anodic, controls, pneumatics, advanced rigging,
oleo legs, tyres. While on the course an opportunity arose to volunteer for flight engineer duties:

> You were accepted providing you passed out with over 50%
> on the fitter's course. I put my name down to become one.
> During my course Catherine came to stay at Shiffnal for a
> couple of weeks. ... We stayed at one of the local pubs and
> very nice it was. When you are living our life in the service,
> doesn't seem half as bad. ... I was sorry when Catherine had
> to go home. I went back into camp.

On 21 October Ferris recorded his new rank as A/C Fitt. 2A and a
65% pass. 'Had to take my props off my blue. Can now become a
Flt/engineer if they want me.' Just over a week later Ferris was posted
to Farnborough, 'the old peace time drome'.

> Parade 7.45 a.m., on the square for flag hoisting and then off
> to work. I worked in the hangars fixing gun mountings on the
> Henleys. Had to do a couple of weeks Backers Up, that goes
> without saying. The hours were fairly reasonable, no guard
> duties for a change. Had a mock raid on the camp in the very

early hours of one dark damp morning. The raid was carried out by the Army and as soon as you were taken prisoner you could go to the Drill Hall for your breakfast. The Army had more than enough prisoners. The RAF Regiment had to stick it out, that's their job anyway.

Called to the Orderly room one morning to be told a signal had come through saying that I should have been at St Athan on my Flt/Eng course last week. What a flap and panic. I've never been cleared off a Station so quick in my life. Even the CO of the flight signed my clearance chit before it was properly completed. As a result I was on my way to St Athan early afternoon.

Ferris started the flight engineer's course at RAF St Athan, Wales, on 27 November. His initial training was on engines, 'Six weeks to do it in. Took the Merlin first then the Bristol radials.' Ferris's next posting was to RAF Stormy Down, 'to learn all about guns and turrets, firing and stripping. It was a very concentrated course, starting at 8 a.m. and ending at 1800 hrs, with duties on top of that, not forgetting our old pal 'guards'. This time we were guarding a back entrance. At least we are improving. If you didn't pass this course you were off the F/Engs course for good, no second trys [sic]. I passed OK with 75%. We had two failures in our entry.' A few days into February 1943 and Ferris was posted back to St Athan to start the final phase of the flight engineer's course. 'Given a choice of aircraft we would like to go on. Lancs, Stirlings or Sunderland flying boats. I asked for Halifax for the simple reason all the Hallie squadrons were in Yorks. Syllabus for course: alighting gear, flying controls, flight engineer duties, cabin heating, fuel system, pyrotechnics, pneumatic system, oxygen system, fire extinguisher system, dinghy equipment, hydraulics, maintenance away from base, pre-flight check, emergency.' Ferris passed with a score of 65%, and promotion followed.

17 March 1943. Change of rank, now Sergeant. ... Issued with the half wing and tapes in the morning, Passing out parade in the afternoon. Pandemonium in the hut whilst everyone busy sewing them on. Passing out parade at 1430 hours complete with band and markers with penants [sic]. ... After the parade kept hanging around for a week or more awaiting posting to a Conversion Unit and joining up with a crew. I've never seen so many airmen (now Sgts.) going around with greatcoats on. I think we all felt very proud of the half wing although we hadn't been airborne yet.

Chapter Three

Ops

As the daylight hours began to lengthen in the early spring of 1943, the war was midway through its fourth year. The Battle of the Atlantic was raging, as German U-boat wolfpacks sent Allied shipping to the ocean floor, seeking to disrupt the shipment of supplies to Britain. There was better news in North Africa where the tide had turned, and on the Eastern front the German Wehrmacht was dealt a shattering blow at Stalingrad. And the Allied air offensive against Germany was set to escalate with Sir Arthur Harris, Commander-in-Chief of Bomber Command, launching what he would call his 'Main Offensive'. The RAF bombing campaign had come a long way since the early days of daylight raids (with resultant unsustainable losses), and the switch to night bombing and the difficulties of finding and hitting targets. In February 1942 a new Air Ministry directive to Bomber Command made it clear that attacks were to focus, 'on the morale of the enemy civil population and in particular the industrial workers'. All and every aspect of Germany's war machine was to be targeted, and new navigation and target-finding aids would become more readily available to assist crews in delivering their bomb loads, from the ever increasing number of four-engined heavy bombers, the Short Stirling, the

Handley Page Halifax and the Avro Lancaster. At the end of May 1942 Harris's 1,000-bomber raid on Cologne proved what his force could be capable of, if given the resources, and by March 1943 an all-out assault on Germany's Ruhr industries was about to be launched. In 1940 and 1941 the enemy had 'sowed the wind'; now, Sir Arthur Harris predicted, they would 'reap the whirlwind'.

Completing his course at the OTU early in March 1943, George recalls, 'We waited to be posted to a squadron and to learn whether we would stay on Wellingtons, still being used operationally at this time, or would convert to the four-engine Halifax or Lancaster, meaning a further course before a squadron posting.' Four-engines it was and a posting to No. 1663 Heavy Conversion Unit at RAF Rufforth, and Handley Page Halifaxes. 'Our crew got to appreciate each other's jobs during this period, and, again, I hammered home the importance of teamwork if we were to survive the next few months. Soon I had my baptism of a first raid over Germany.' To give fledgling pilots operational experience they would be detailed to accompany an operational squadron pilot and crew as second pilot, or, as it was known, second 'dickey'.

> Shortly after arriving at the HCU at Rufforth, and before my feet had hardly touched the ground they said, 'You are to go off to No. 10 Squadron at Melbourne and do your two second dickey trips.
>
> When I went to the squadron briefing it was all strange to me. I hadn't even set foot in a Halifax. The first trip, where would it be? Essen, home of the Krupps works.
>
> I was apprehensive, but the crew that I went with, I sensed that they were a good crew. The flight engineer said to me, 'That second dickey seat is mine for take off and landing. You can have the in between bit.'
>
> We went off, no trouble, but I couldn't believe what I was seeing when we got over the target. The flak was unbelievable.

It was certainly an eye-opener and I thought, 'My God if it is going to be like this we need to be lucky.' The following night was a trip to Kiel which again was quite a heavily defended target. I was glad to get them under my belt, but when I went back to the Heavy Conversion Unit my crew said to me, 'Well what was it like? Were you frightened?' I said, 'Well if we are going to get through this, we have got to do it together. And, put it this way, when you pack your gear to go on our first trip remember to take a spare pair of underpants.

The conversion to four engines required the aforementioned additions to the crew, Joe Scrivener as air gunner, and a flight engineer. Apart from his engineering capabilities George had another well-founded reason to welcome his new crew member: 'In regard [to] our flight engineer it was a question of accepting the next in line, who turned out to be Ferris Newton from Horsforth near Leeds. This was again fortunate for us as his mother and wife ran a pub, The Old Ball (or 'knackered bollock') in Horsforth, and often all seven of us piled into the Morris 8 owned by Ferris, four in the back and three in the front, and carried out sorties to the pub, where the locals treated us very generously. The worst part was getting up next morning for an hour and half drive back to base.'

Ferris's first impressions on arrival at No. 1663 Heavy Conversion Unit were, 'Not a bad place. War time aerodrome of course.'

Not too far out of York. After getting settled in, went with the other F/Engs to the CO's office to get put in a crew. I was about sixth in the queue, and later I was to remember it, in fact I've never forgotten it, that was the queue the 'Reaper' had his eyes on. He made his selection along with the CO, but His was for keeps. Both the engineer in front and behind were killed along with their respective crews very soon after they were operational.

I was told that I should be put in Sgt Dunn's crew, so off

I went to the Mess at lunch time to find Sgt Dunn. Met George, told him I was going to be in his crew, so he introduced me to the rest. Sgt Dean (Dixie) rear gunner, Sgt Todd (Jock) wireless operator, Sgt Maitland (Andy) bomb aimer. The other two members of the crew were both Officers so I should meet them later.

On 14 April 1943 Ferris made his first flight in a Halifax, with an instructor pilot and George in the second pilot's seat. 'I went up without an instructor engineer.'

I managed but certainly felt very strange. It was only a weather test in any case. Second flight was at 1535 for circuits and landings. The instructor was the Flight Commander Flt/Lt Woodhatch.

During the course of the flying the electric horn would keep buzzing, making it very difficult for F/Lt Woodhatch to give George instructions. So up pops a voice, 'Pilot to engineer, please stop horn blowing.' Just for a few seconds I felt awful. My goodness what had I been told – fuses – hundreds of them. Then I remembered fuse box number 18, number 20 fuse. Down I went to the fuse panel, pulled out the fuse and hoped for the best. It worked.

On the next day we were doing some circuits and bumps. Then on the third or fourth landing the starboard tyre burst. Lucky for us it was not done on take-off. We might have been a write-off. On the 18th we practised three-engine flying for which I was truly thankful when it was over. However on the 21st we did two-engine flying, so I needn't have worried before. Anyway it gave us all a bit more confidence (later we used to do one-engine flying). The same day as we did the two-engine flying we did air/sea firing and bombing. I had to go in the rear turret firing a few rounds into the sea. I didn't feel at all comfy in the turret, always had a feeling that it would snap off from the rest of the aircraft.

Three days later Ferris had his first experience of a fighter affiliation flight, 'the nearest a large four-engine bomber gets to doing aerobatics. Very good practice for the gunners and pilot but the rest of the crew just hang on and feel sick.'

> The next day we went off as a crew on a cross-country flight, which lasted 5 hours 50 minutes. I held up take-off declaring that we hadn't enough petrol in the tanks. Woodhatch came tearing round in his car to know why the hell we hadn't taken off yet. 'Short of petrol', says engineer. 'Get in the aircraft and I'll see you tomorrow', said the flight commander. Next day George and I on the mat, he tore us off a strip.
>
> On the 27th we started the last phase of our final training before going operational, that is night flying circuits and bumps, finishing up with a night cross-country of 5 hours 30 minutes. On the cross-country one of the towns we had to pass over was Bristol and as we were approaching our search light gave us warning of an enemy raid taking place there, so off we shot in the other direction as quick as we could. No point in getting in the flak. One of our kites got caught in the balloon barrage. Total hours flown at the conversion unit 60 hours.

Having successfully got to grips with the four-engined Halifax, George's crew was posted to No. 76 Squadron, which had the motto 'Resolute'. Based at RAF Linton-on-Ouse, No. 76 shared the base with No. 78 Squadron, George recalling: 'The officers lived in quarters on the camp and the NCOs were billeted in Beningbrough Hall, a stately home near the airfield and home of Lady Chesterfield prior to requisitioning by the RAF.' Andy Maitland wrote: 'The house stood in beautiful grounds on the banks of the River Ouse and oh how wonderful it was to walk by the river and try and forget the horrors of war.' George recently had occasion to revisit the Hall.

The estate is now administered by the National Trust and in October 2019 while visiting Linton, just prior to its closure, and the Yorkshire Air Museum at Elvington, I took the opportunity of renewing my acquaintance with Beningbrough Hall. I received a very warm welcome from the staff and was given a tour of the hall where I found the décor in much better shape than in 1943. Much to the surprise of the staff I was able to give them a few snippets of information that they had not heard of, particularly about the Blue Room where my crew were billeted, and told them that we were ferried across the nearby river by a boatman so that we could visit the local pub, the Alice Hawthorn. I was asked if I knew anything about two statues which were in the grounds in 1943 but had somehow disappeared in the ensuing years, but on this occasion, I pleaded not guilty!

Having arrived at RAF Linton-on-Ouse in May 1943, George now prepared his crew for operations against the enemy. His leadership style would be key to their success and survival, which he describes as fairly firm. George recounts an example of his approach in regard to one of their operational raids.

On one occasion the navigator Reg, a good navigator, came up and said 'We're miles to port.' I said, 'We can't be Reg. I've been rigidly sticking to the course that you gave me. We can't be miles to port.' He said, 'Well we are.' He seemed to have lost it, momentarily. I said, 'Reg, get your bloody finger out. Get yourself a fix. If you can't do the job I'll get Andy to take over. I'm going to steer ten degrees starboard, if you say we are way off to port, to get us back on what you say we should be. In the meantime get yourself a fix.' With that he suddenly came to and everything was alright. He apologised when we got when we got home, for momentarily going a bit haywire. I was always insisting that they keep a good look out. All the time. Every now and then I'd be saying 'Are you awake Dixie?' You had to be. Although I was only a sergeant, I had control of the aircraft, even though there were officers on the crew. We had one particular fellow on the squadron who had a reputation for turning back. In fact he was called 'Turnabout ****'. Eventually he was shipped off to the punishment camp at Sheffield. I could be sympathetic up to a point. But you said to yourself if I'm prepared to do it why can't they.

Ferris recorded his arrival at RAF Linton-on-Ouse and No. 76 Squadron: 'A peace time camp, there was only one snag and that was we had two squadrons operating from there, 76 and 78. Too many of course for one station, the result being 76 personnel were billeted at Beningbrough Hall about three miles away, for which we were issued with bikes. Later I got my car running again, now being operational I was entitled to petrol.' In the second week of May George spent a few days carrying out beam approach training at No. 1502 BAT Flight, RAF Driffield, and while he was away Ferris and the rest of the crew enjoyed some leave. On return Ferris reported to his section and discovered, 'I was reserve engineer. Next day the Tannoy was calling for Sergeant Newton to report to engineer section. My worst fears were correct, an engineer had gone sick and I had to take his place that night. Sergeant Myers was the pilot, an Aussie, so I looked him up in the mess and told him I was his engineer for that night.' That afternoon Ferris went to check on his aircraft. And a word here about the groundcrew and the part they play:

It is the duty of the ground crew to keep the aircraft serviceable. Their importance is therefore very great. The success of the attack and the lives of the flying crews depend on them. As soon as an aircraft lands for a night sortie the duty crew covers its engines and turrets. At daylight the ground crew consisting of two fitters, and rigger, go over all the aircraft from nose to tail. The wings and fuselage are checked for holes caused by flak. The bomb racks are examined and an electrician checks all the electrical gear, paying particular attention to the bomb release gear. Controls are tested, hydraulics, brakes, and oxygen system, tyres checked, etcetera. The whole process takes about three hours.

Once the orders for a raid have been received at the station, the ground crews begin the fuelling and bombing up. Sufficient petrol to see the bomber to the target and back, with a safety margin, is carried, and bombs are brought in on a trolley, pulled by a tractor, from the bomb dump. These trains visit each aircraft and the bombs are transferred. Portable cranes are used and the bombs which have already been fused at the dump are slung into position. They are attached to the aircraft by means of lugs and are released by an electro-magnetic system which is controlled by switches operated by the bomb-aimer (this switchboard was called Mickey Mouse). Bombing up with bombs of a thousand pounds or over is not easy and requires skill, practice and team work. An expert bombing up squad of twenty-eight men can load fifteen aircraft in two hours.

On 13 May 1943 Ferris prepared for his first operation against the enemy. Seventeen Halifaxes from No. 76 Squadron were detailed to take part in the raid on Bochum.

Went back to the Mess to try and eat the special meal put on. I had a very funny feeling in my tummy ever since I had been told I was going that night. I was curious and anxious at the same time to know how I would react in the face of danger, and to know what it was really like on the other side. Anyway not long to wait now. Briefing – we moved in small silent groups down to the Intelligence room. First a room cluttered up with

photos, maps, chairs, technical papers, and confidential Air
Ministry publications. In the wall another door giving access
to the briefing room. The atmosphere caught you by the
throat the moment you put your foot inside the door. The
first thing you saw was the big map nearly covering the whole
of the wall behind the platform. The great big splashes of red
covering defended areas and the part left white the undefended.
Every time the CO used to say 'We have routed you through
the gap in the Ruhr', everyone used to give a nervous laugh.

A red ribbon joins Linton with a turning point in Norfolk,
then straight across the North Sea over the Dutch coast and
on into Germany to Bochum, a town in the Ruhr (Happy
Valley it used to be called). From Bochum the ribbon turned
coming North over the Friesian Islands and back over the
North Sea, crossing the English coast around Bridlington.
After taking in the target and route one settles down feeling a
little better, especially as it wasn't too bad a target – could
have been Berlin or Essen. The next thing to worry about
was a blackboard set up on the right of the platform with the
weather drawn on it. What was it going to do? Clear on take-
off, bad on landing that would in all probability mean a
diversion to some other drome, and that was always a bind.
Was it going to be clear or cloudy on the other side? Whether
there was much cloud on the way over with a possibility of
icing. I was always very nervous of the weather, and on the
two occasions when I was really scared stiff, they were both
due to weather conditions.

After briefing the big wait for the take-off. There is nothing
harder to kill than TIME. Down to the locker rooms to
change. Empty pockets, thick socks, flying boots, white
pullover under battle dress blouse, scarf round neck, put on
parachute harness, Mae West, sweets, chewing gum, tin of
orange juice, flask of coffee. That's about the lot. The gunners
have electrically heated flying suits. The Signal cartridges,

message pad, torch, flimsies on which is typed the procedure
to be adopted if the aircraft is lost or forced down. The flimsies
are made of rice paper so that they can be destroyed by eating
them. The taste of ink leaves much to be desired. In another
pocket, protractor, dividers, coloured pencils, course and
speed calculator, log book, target map, and a questionnaire
to be filled in for the benefit of the Met man. Also Astro
navigator tables.

Somebody shouts crew bus and we all stagger out
looking like a lot of men from Mars. Everybody laughing
and shouting, but I think they all felt like I did inside.

'A' for Apple, this is my kite for tonight. Go through the
pre-flight check, everything in its place. Get out again and
join rest of crew laying around on the grass, all waiting for
start-up time. The Wingco came around in his car to see if
everything is OK. 23.20 start-up, pilot and engineer get in,
another final quick check, then into position. Ground crew
standing by outside. Contact port inner. Contact port outer.
Contact starboard outer. Contact starboard inner. Run up,
test the mags, check oil pressure and temperature. … Rest of
crew in by now, one of the ground crew bring form 700 for
the pilot to sign. I follow him down to the exit and close it.
'Engineer to Pilot rear hatch closed and secure OK to taxi.'

Pilot signals chocks away to ground crew and we start
to roll forward to join up with the rest of the aircraft waiting
to take off. Whilst this has been going off the wireless op has
been checking his wireless. He does this by speaking to the
Watch Office as follows, 'Hullo Parsnip', codename for the
station, 'Hullo Parsnip, G for George calling are you receiving
me, are you receiving me. Over to you.' If all is well the
Watch Office will reply, 'Parsnip answering G George. Parsnip
answering G George. I am receiving you loud and clear
strength niner.' All sentences are repeated sentence by sentence
to be sure they are properly understood.

'A' Apple's turn for take-off, swing onto runway, clear
engines, 'Engineer to pilot OK for take-off rad shutters
closed.' There goes the green light from the A.C.P and with a
loud roar the kite slowly gathers speed. Revs 3,000 + 12 lbs
boost the tail comes up first and by the time we are doing 90–
100 mph we are practically airborne. At 125 IAS reduce revs to
2,850 + 9 lbs boost and begin the climb to operational height,
for Halifax aircraft usually about 18,000 feet. Navigator gives
first course to steer by and we are on our way. On reaching
the coast the navigator pinpoints his position, giving the
necessary direction to bring the aircraft dead on course.
Navigation lights go out. Very pistol loaded with colour of
the day. Over the sea the bomb-aimer makes the bombs live.
Inside the aircraft there is darkness, engineer checks the
blackout. The luminous paint on the dials and instruments
shows up very clear. Back in the rear turret the gunner has
settled down in his seat. The turret is power operated and
swings easily in any direction. First he tests it moving it to and
fro. Then he loads and cocks the guns. This done he switches
over his intercom and reports to the pilot everything OK, the
mid-upper gunner going through the same procedure.

The next hour or so pass quietly. Nobody speaks as the aircraft slowly gains height. At 10,000 feet put on oxygen, and by
15,000 feet we are well out over the sea and approaching the
enemy coast. As we pass over it light flak comes up from flak
ships or coast defence batteries. Nothing much to worry
about, as a lot of it can't reach our height. Away in the
distance searchlights start probing the sky and more flak
becomes visible. The PFF boys have been there just ahead of
us and now you can see the whole of the target nicely marked
out with red and green markers. As the target is coming up
the whole of the sky seems to be full of searchlights and
I remember thinking to myself that we should never get
through that lot without being caught in a light.

An extract from Wing Commander Smith's report: 'They (searchlights) were everywhere, in some places unbroken walls of them. We were in the early part of the raid and it was obvious by the way the searchlights wavered about at Cologne, Duisburg, and Düsseldorf, that they had no idea where the attack was going to develop. It was as light as day and the whole Ruhr valley seemed to be lit up by the moon and search lights. Near Bochum itself there must have been fifteen large cones with between thirty and forty beams in each. The lights would wave about until they found somebody. Then all the beams in the area would fasten on to that aircraft and shells would be pumped up the cone. We could see bombers held like that a long way ahead.'

Now the heavy flak is exploding all around. At the moment it is just barrage stuff, nothing predicted. On the bombing run the bomb-aimer takes charge, guiding the aircraft to bring his bomb sight over a red marker. Engineer changes onto full petrol tanks and stands by to open bomb doors. Bomb doors open, engineer goes back into position and keeps a sharp look out through the astra dome for enemy fighters. Everyone keyed up. Aircraft is put in a shallow dive to go across target. Bomb-aimer gives pilot left or right as a marker comes into bomb sight. You feel a slight jar as the bombs go, and that's it. Everyone feels much better when the bombs [have] gone. The bombing run can be sticky as you are keeping a straight course (or should be) and that gives the enemy radar a good chance of picking up a good plot of your range.

As the bomb-aimer presses the bomb tit a photo flash flare is automatically released and the camera takes a photo. This enables intelligence to assess and, if possible, plot the position of the aircraft in relation to aiming point (if there is any ground detail of course). The navigator gives next course to pilot and we carry on hoping for the best. After the target area there is nothing much happening, the odd search light here and there and a little flak in the distance. As the coast comes up there is the light flak again and when that is passed there is a general easing of tension. Some of the knots in your tummy seem to undo. The aircraft is put into a slow decent for the English Coast. At 10,000 feet oxygen masks can be removed and it's about time for a drink of coffee. This is most welcome as one's mouth feels like the bottom of a bird cage. That's the oxygen.

By 8,000 feet we pass over the coast and lose more height fairly quickly. The time is now nearly four a.m. and everyone starts looking for Linton beacon flashing its welcoming red light. There it is. Call up base on RT and get permission to land. Pilot calls up and we hear we are number seven to land. That will mean nearly thirty minutes circling base waiting our turn to land. At last it is our turn, wheels and flaps down, final approach, touch down, taxi round to dispersal, switch off, and it's all over. Only another 29 times to go through that and I've finished.

It had been a good night for No. 76 Squadron. Although two aircraft had returned early owing to technical problems, the remaining fifteen Halifaxes reached the target and bombed it. Whether they hit the target is a matter of conjecture. *The Bomber Command War Diaries* records that the Germans lit decoy markers, which attracted much of the bombing. Other squadrons had not fared as well as No. 76, with twenty-four aircraft lost.

Ferris, following his first operation, was optimistic.

Flying time for the trip was 5 hours 35 min, not bad for a breaking in. From the aircraft the crew bus takes us round to be debriefed. It's a very free and easy affair, hot tea and biscuits are served by the WAAFs (bless 'em). The CO and Flight Commanders, Section Leaders, are always there. The AOC

pops in sometimes, perhaps if it has been a special raid. After
that it's to the Mess for bacon and eggs and then off to bed
hoping you will not be on again tonight. Usually you do two
on and one off.

I was now the first member of our crew apart from George
who had done a trip, so of course the next morning I was
plied with questions from the rest of the crew. Told them they
wouldn't have long to wait.

Ferris was right. On 23rd May George's crew was detailed to take
part in a raid on Dortmund, one of 826 crews manning Lancasters,
Halifaxes, Wellington, Stirlings and Mosquitoes. For Andy
Maitland, 'this was the day we had trained for and our war effort
was about to commence. I remember thinking perhaps I should be
more excited but I seemed to be looking forward to finding out
what it was all about over Europe and to find out for myself just
how frightening an experience it would be. … I felt on this first
operation, as I did on all my later sorties, that the period just prior
to take-off was always most tense. Once airborne, there was so
much to attend to that one forgot the tensions and concentrated
on the job in hand.'

Ferris already knew first-hand what it was like flying in hostile
skies, as did George; the rest of the crew were now to discover exactly
how keen the Germans were to defend their armament 'foundry',
with the skies above swept with scores of searchlights and the area
bristling with anti-aircraft guns. George recalls, 'One wonders how
it was possible to not get hit.'

Often the target was located in the heavily defended Ruhr, a
fact that would be revealed to expectant crews at briefing,
where, upon arrival the target for that night was hidden from
the crews behind a curtain. When you walked in the main
concern was what the target was going to be. When they drew
the curtain back you saw the red ribbon crossing Europe. 'Oh

not the Ruhr again.' You had the Met officer, the navigation officer, the gunnery officer – all gave their spiel. At the end of the briefing you were pretty well informed as to where the defences were likely to be heavy, the route in – they tried to route you to clear many of the heavy ack-ack places. Then the navigator and captain had a separate briefing, after the main briefing.

Our first sortie as a crew took place on the night of 23 May 1943 and was to Dortmund, in the Ruhr. The flak was vicious and accurate.

Ferris remembered: 'Flying time for the trip was 7 hours 5 minutes and the reason why it was all that time was the fact that on returning to base we found ourselves about number 16 to land. That meant that there were too many aircraft on the circuit so we were sent off on what was called the Dog Leg. That was going as far as Scarborough and back, even then we were well up the list for landing. Having two squadrons on one station was of course too much for it to handle.'

Landing back at base at 05.32hrs, George taxied the Halifax back to its dispersal point. Andy Maitland commented: 'What a great feeling to be alive and oh how very good that cigarette tasted as we chatted to our ground staff and climbed on to the crew bus which would take us round the perimeter track to the hangars where we could return our safety equipment and then it would be on to debriefing.'

From the attacking force that night thirty-eight aircraft were lost, including two from No. 76 Squadron, that of Flight Sergeant Bawden, the pilot and two of his crew being killed, and also Sergeant Cousins who was well known to George:

Cliff Cousins, a good friend who trained with me in Canada, was shot down and his two gunners were killed. Cliff survived and became a prisoner-of-war and I was privileged to be the best man at his wedding on his return after the war.

It may sound callous, but you got used to the empty beds next to you. You would go down to flights and it would be, 'Oh he didn't make it back last night.' You would probably find you were on that night, so you didn't have a lot of time to mull over the loss.

Late on 25 May, at 23.45hrs, George lifted Halifax DK148 'J' from the Linton runway, destined for Düsseldorf, attacking at 01.57hrs from 19,000 feet. George's entry in the squadron's Operations Record Book (ORB) recording: 'As aircraft approached T/A [target area] a red marker was seen on the run-up and bombs were released. A number of fires were seen ... and some buildings were seen blazing ... smoke rising to 17,000 ft.'

On 27 May the target, as recorded by Ferris, was 'the celebrated Essen'. Take-off was 22.47hrs, with a bomb-release time recorded at 01.16hrs, a little later than expected.

Very heavy flak greeted us. I remember poor old Reg getting in a bit of a flap about our position saying he was lost. A most unusual statement for him to make as he was one of the best navigators on the squadron. George told him to pull his finger out and give him a course, which he did more or less straight away, and put us back on track. The gunners were jumpy as well and George told them off. It was due to nerves as we were all very much keyed up that night.

For the night of 29/30 May the target was Wuppertal, Ferris noting, 'to add to the general confusion in that area as the Dam Busters had just been over. Wuppertal lay in the path of the flood waters.' (The famous No. 617 Squadron raid on the Ruhr dams had taken place on the night of 16/17 May 1943.) The ORB entry for George's crew noted that they bombed on the markers, with the city below lit by a sizeable concentration of fires and a 'large orange explosion'.

The Bomber Command War Diaries record the raid as 'the outstanding success of the Battle of the Ruhr', with widespread devastation. The cost to Bomber Command, from the 719 aircraft despatched on the raid, was 33 aircraft, but the No. 76 Squadron diarist could state, 'All our aircraft returned safely.'

The next raids for George and his crew were on 11 and 12 June, Ferris remembering 'the first to Düsseldorf and the other to Bochum, both second visits. At Düsseldorf the search lights were operating in large cones (makes a change). Bochum still had the largest concentration of search lights I'd ever seen anywhere up to then. Again we went through it all without getting caught.' Other crews from No. 76 Squadron had not been so fortunate, initially recorded as 'failed to return' awaiting news of their fate. Andy Maitland recollected: 'This was when the reality of war struck home and one wondered were the missing crew members lying dead or wounded in a foreign land, trying to escape, or taken prisoner of war. These were the permutations and all I hoped was that they were alive.' Three Halifaxes failed to return across the raids of 11 and 12 June, with sixteen lives lost and five men captured.

In the middle of June No. 76 Squadron transferred to RAF Holme-on-Spalding-Moor to the south-east of York. With the expansion of the Royal Canadian Air Force No. 6 Group, their respective squadrons were to have the benefit of the better facilities offered by the pre-war stations such as RAF Linton-on-Ouse. George and many of his RAF squadron crew colleagues now made way for their Commonwealth friends. (If this was done graciously or not will be unreported in the interests of international goodwill.) Ferris recalled:

On the 16 June the whole squadron moved to Holme-on-Spalding-Moor. Our sister squadron, No. 78, went to Breighton, a few miles away. Whilst turning round in dispersal caught the starboard wing tip on a tall hedge. New wing tip required. Nothing was said about it but I always thought that I should

have given a quicker warning to George and perhaps have
saved it.

Holme-on-Spalding-Moor. Funny I should get back here as
aircrew. I left here in March 1942. Got settled in and the first
op from here was to Krefeld on 21 June. This was a fairly easy
target, not many defences and flying was 4 hours 25 mins,
which turned out to be the shortest op we ever did.

No. 76 Squadron was fortunate to have no losses on the Krefeld raid,
but not so on the following night's attack on Mülheim, in which
George, Ferris and crew took part. Following a night fighter attack
Pilot Officer Carrie ordered his crew to bail out from their mortally
wounded Halifax. Tragically Sergeant Huke's parachute failed to
deploy – the rest of the crew survived and were captured.

For the raid to Wuppertal on the night of 24/25 June, Ferris
recounted:

At the next briefing that our kite was down for doing special
reconnaissance. This means that in addition to normal bombing
we had to do a stooge round and have a good look at what
was happening. Each crew got this job in turn, after completing
a few raids and got a little experience. The target was our old
friends Wuppertal, second visit. We had been routed through
the so called gap on the Ruhr defences, and I remember
thinking how active it was to say there were no guns there.

One No. 76 Squadron Halifax fell to the flak that night, Canadian
Flight Lieutenant Cheetham losing his life along with two of his crew.

For the raid to Gelsenkirchen on the 25th, No. 76 Squadron
detailed seventeen of their Halifaxes, including George's. But the
night did not start well. Only sixteen were able to take off and then
five were forced to return early owing to technical problems.
George's and ten other crews did reach the target, which was covered
in 10/10 cloud, Andy Maitland releasing the bombs from 20,000

feet at 01.29hrs, their ORB entry recording, 'Orange coloured explosion in the target area at 0121 hours.' Ferris recalled the use of Pathfinder 'Wanganui' sky markers that night: 'The target was completely covered by cloud. The markers were supposed to hang in the sky, but whether they stayed over the target was another matter. It was a new experience to bomb and not see anything but a layer of cloud. Of course the old flak popped up back at you, but the searchlights were ineffective.' Not so on the next raid, to Cologne, on 28 June. As George remembers, it was when he first encountered 'one of the fears shared by all crews, getting coned'. Take-off time was 23.10hrs, and within two and three-quarter hours George's Halifax was on the bomb run.

[Ferris:] Of course the Cathedral was carefully avoided, every one going down just to make sure they didn't hit it. The way that place was plastered with bombs and the Cathedral remained standing is a miracle.

[George:] After leaving the target a batch of searchlights suddenly went out and I sensed a trap. The next minute we were picked up by a blue radar-controlled searchlight and a whole host of white searchlights joined it.

[Ferris:] George seemed to sense something like a trap, and he had just given us all an alert when SNAP – master search light on us first time. These master lights were controlled by radar. Then up came three or four other beams and we were coned.

[George:] We were like a fairy sitting on top of a Christmas tree, a sitting duck for any night fighters that were around.

[Ferris:] George kept his head well down and concentrated on his flying instruments, taking violent evasive action. It's a mistake to look out as of course you are blinded by the beam and then you can't see a thing. Having now got us coned up comes the flak.

[George:] The only way to get out of this situation was to use a corkscrew manoeuvre, a series of dives and climbing turns, but even that did not always work. It takes some effort to heave a heavy aircraft around and the pilot has to avoid looking outside and getting blinded. Suddenly there was a heavy burst of flak in front of us, followed by two others on both sides of the aircraft.

[Ferris:] The first burst seemed to be dead in front of the nose, the next was just off the port wing, and the third was just a hell of a clatter and bang, shook the old kite up a bit, made my hair stand on end, turning my tummy over at the same time and that was that.

It seems like hours before you fly out of the beams, but George was taking some very useful evasive action, and we had shaken one or two of the lights off, then the master light went out, and everything was back to normal.

Having wrestled his Halifax through the corkscrew and having managed to shake off the searchlights, George instructed Ferris 'to inspect for damage that felt quite serious'. Ferris began his check,

[Ferris:] … to see if there was any damage to any of the pipes, hydraulics, petrol, oxygen, etc., inside the aircraft, but there was none that could be seen in the air.

Judging by the noise at the time of the attack we expected to see the bomb doors blown off or a large gaping hole, so imagine our surprise on landing and all getting out to try and find the hole. Actually there were only a dozen or so small holes, so what it must be like to be really shot up I wouldn't know.

[Andy Maitland:] This was the first time our aircraft had been hit and the nearest we had come to being shot from the sky so one can well imagine the look of relief on our faces as we climbed down from the aircraft steps on to terra firma. When we got to debriefing, never was coffee to taste so good as we sat down at the table to relate our story of the raid.

The squadron ORB records George as having a second dickie on this raid, Sergeant Rogerson. Quite some entry into the air war. Two No. 76 Squadron crews failed to return from the raid, Sergeant Parritt's and Sergeant Coles's, with a total loss of life.

On 3 July, Ferris recorded: 'As we missed the Cathedral last time they decided to send us again. The flak was very intense with about three tenths cloud cover over the target.' This was Ferris's thirteenth operation, something he and the crew felt was in need of celebrating, 'by all coming over to the O.B. [Old Ball]'

I'm afraid I was a sick man before I went to bed. I tried to drink thirteen whiskies but my tummy gave in before me. Everyone said my face was first green then white and back to green.

(I must have looked as a traffic light.) I tried to eat my supper of fish and chips (heaven help me) but I couldn't make it. Went off to bed to die. Anyway a good time was had by all.

Went back to work and the next one [9/10 July] was our old pal Gelsenkirchen, and very hot it was, they didn't half put up a barrage that night. How on earth we could fly through it and not get hit, it used to beat me. ... Took Sergeant Hoverstad, one of his second pilot trips. The barrage rather shook him I'm afraid. Shook us as well but we didn't tell him that. This trip was a tour round France as well. A new idea to try and fool Jerrie [sic]. They used to say it cut the losses, but we have only the Boffins for that. We used to fly in from the North Sea over Holland into Germany and instead of coming back more or less the same way, we would carry on into France and

across the Channel coming over our coast around Beachy
Head then straight up the Midlands to base. That made the
flying time 6 hours 5 minutes as against 4 hours 30 minutes.

For the next raid, George would again be accompanied by a second
pilot, No. 76 Squadron detailing twenty-four aircraft to take part
in the raid on Aachen. Ferris recounted:

July 13th, ops on. Word used to come through from Group
in the morning, and by lunch time you knew who was going
and who wasn't. If you were on you usually went down to the
kite, see whether they were fitting long range petrol tanks or
what sort of bomb load it was going to be. Other days we
had some very interesting lectures to attend. Perhaps a talk by
some chap who had baled out and walked back, contacting
the Underground and all that. They gave us some very useful
tips on what to do and not to do. Other interesting talks were
given by our interrogators of German POWs. How a little bit
of information given was nothing on its own but with another
little bit given by somebody else, made more information
for us. One could learn quite a lot from those little talks,
very useful.

   We all carried escape kit and also money in a sealed packet.
These two items had of course to be handed in after each trip,
engineer being responsible for same. Joe, our mid-upper
gunner always used to take a civilian jacket and trousers with
him and to make matters worse for himself he carried a small
revolver. If he had been caught on the other side with all that
he would have been shot as a spy and no questions asked. We
all used to try and put him off taking them but it was no good.
Other times we used to get the crew together for dinghy drill,
go out to the aircraft and go through all the drill for ditching.

   Dinghy Drill. Captain on deciding to ditch will give order
'Dinghy Dinghy prepare for ditching', to which each member

of crew will reply 'Engineer ditching sir.' Engineer will check Captain securely fastened in his seat, Sutton harness tight.

Captain then gives order 'Dinghy dinghy crash positions', and go aft to assist mid-upper gunner to remove emergency packs from their clips and to open rear upper escape hatch. He will then assume crash position which is seated on floor facing aft with back braced.

On first impact of tail touching water it must not be mistaken for final impact and no relaxation should be allowed before second impact, when aircraft will come to rest (we hope).

After ditching Engineer will pull manual release and attach rescue line to his waist. He will leave aircraft first (loud cheers) and enter dinghy and accept equipment from crew.

We got our drill down to about 15 seconds, every one out and in the dinghy.

The dinghy is stowed in the Port main plane and will inflate itself automatically from a CO_2 bottle stowed with it, on inflation it will release itself from the stowage in the wing.

If you have had time for your wireless op to send out an SOS and last known position you should be picked up by the Air Sea Rescue boys fairly quickly. Nowhere was too far for them, they have been known to go over to the enemy coast to pick a crew up out of the drink. If no wireless message was sent then at first light you would send your pigeon with a message. If your pigeon was killed or drowned then you would use the portable wireless (a small kite provided to get an aerial up).

To go back to the 13th, the target was Aachen and we were first wave in. There were no searchlights and very little flak. We were ahead of time so had to do an orbit before starting the bombing run. Never did like doing an orbit, always used to have a fear of bumping into one of our aircraft coming on in another wave. Anyway everything passed off alright, flying time for the trip 5 hours 5 minutes. This was another tour of France on the way back.

George, Ferris and crew, that night, were able to report their experience of the raid on return to RAF Holme-on-Spalding-Moor. Of the twenty-four crews detailed for the raid only thirteen could do similarly. The undercarriage of the Halifax piloted by Lieutenant Hulthin, RNAF, collapsed as they were taxying along the runway preparing for take-off. The aircraft was engulfed in flames, but fortunately the crew made a rapid exit and there were no casualties. The ten Halifaxes that were not yet airborne were forced to stand down.

George's seventeenth operational sortie, on the night of 15/16 July 1943, was somewhat unusual. A raid to the Peugeot motor factory in the Montbéliard suburb of Sochaux, on the French side of the border with Switzerland. The No. 76 Squadron diarist recorded: 'Never in the history of this squadron have so many aircraft been detailed to take off in operations against the enemy. Twenty-three were detailed and all took off successfully in good time.' Ferris recalled:

The defences of the factory were weak. Whether Jerrie [sic] thought it would never be attacked I don't know, but apart from one or two search lights and some light flak some of which was situated on the roof of all places, there was nothing to worry about. From our point of view it was a perfect raid. We were the first on the target and you could actually see the factory as we were down to 4,000 feet. Our bombing run had just started and the first red marker was just going down. PFF boys bang on the job and G for George bombing practically to the second. One minute peace and joy and as our bombs and incendiaries hit the factory Hell let loose. As we turned to our new course the whole of the factory seemed to be enveloped in flames. The roof had gone and those Jerries manning the guns had gone with it. By this time more flak had opened up and it was fairly whistling past us, but we managed to avoid being hit. One or two of the boys were caught by German

night fighters on the way back up France. Andy took quite
a few Astro shots on the way back; he had also got a good
photo of the aiming point. Flying time for the trip 7 hours
55 minutes.

The No. 76 Squadron diarist was similarly optimistic about the
results of the raid, stating that crews had the 'satisfaction of seeing
their bombs straddle the works. … The attack which was carried
out from an average of 7,500 feet appeared to be well concentrated
and fires and explosions were observed. The entire target area
seemed to be a mass of flame.' However, *The Bomber Command War
Diaries* note that the Pathfinder markers were off target and most
of the bombing had fallen in the town, with the factory assessed
as only 5% damaged.

Two weeks' leave followed the Montbéliard raid, and while
George was away he recalls:

On the night of 25/26 July my aircraft was being flown by
Flight Lieutenant Shannon RAAF on a raid to Essen.
Unfortunately, one of the engines shed a propeller and the
blades flew into the forward fuselage causing a gaping hole
and untold damage. In the confusion the mid-upper gunner
bailed out and others were about to do the same when
Shannon got the aircraft under control and was able to get
it back to Holme and carry out a belly landing without any
casualties.

As the month of July was drawing to a close, with leave over, Ferris
remembered that they 'Got back in time to take part in the concentrated raids on Hamburg.'

Chapter Four

Whirlwind

On the night of 4/5 April 1943, George had flown his second-dickey trip with No. 10 Squadron to Kiel. That same night in the North Atlantic, German *U-boat 229*, which had been laid down at F. Krupp Germaniawerft AG, Kiel, in November 1941, fired a torpedo at the Swedish motor merchant vessel the *Vaalaren*. The ship sank and, although there is a German report that a lifeboat was seen, all the crew and passengers, forty-five lives, were lost. April 1943 proved a bad month for Allied shipping with U-boats responsible for the loss of forty-nine ships (totalling 226,274 tons) and eight ships were damaged (totalling 56,270 tons). Many of these U-boats had been laid down in shipyards located in Hamburg, and notable examples of sinkings caused by Hamburg U-boats include:

4/5 April 1943, *U-635* and *U-630* were involved in the sinking of the *Shillong*, a motor merchant vessel, with seventy-one killed.

5 April 1943, *U-530* and *U-563* were involved in the sinking of the *Sunoil*, a motor tanker vessel, with all sixty-nine people on board killed.

11 April 1943, *U-615* sank the *Edward B. Dudley*, a steam

merchant ship, killing the entire crew of sixty-nine.
20 April 1943, *U-565* sank the *Sidi-Bel-Abbès*, a troop transport.
Senegalese troops were on board and 611 lives were lost.

The excellent uboat.net website provides a detailed analysis of the
U-boat campaign, and states that from a total U-boat production
of 1,156, the following were from Hamburg shipyards: Blohm & Voss
(224), Deutsche Werft AG (113), H.C. Stülcken Sohn (24), Howaldts-
werke Hamburg AG (33). This equates to 34% of German U-boats
being laid down in Hamburg shipyards. It is hardly surprising, therefore, that Hamburg would be subjected to aerial bombardment.

In July and August 1943, Hamburg would be targeted in one of
the most devastating bombing attacks of the war. Allied commanders had a simple choice: leave the expansion of the German wolfpacks unchecked or try and destroy the U-boats in their nests,
relieving pressure on the Navy, Merchant and Royal, in the Atlantic.
No. 76 Squadron took part in the first and second attacks of the
Battle of Hamburg, losing one crew on 24/25 July 1943, and a further
Halifax severely mauled by night fighters on 27/28 July, with the
mid-upper gunner killed. Notable on the first of these raids was the
introduction of Window, metallic strips dropped in great numbers
by crews and proving successful in clouding and confusing German
radar. It was the raid of 27/28 July that caused the devastating
firestorm, resulting in tens of thousands of German casualties. Sir
Arthur Harris's 'whirlwind' had swept through Hamburg.

By 29 July George, Ferris and crew were back from leave. Ferris recalled, 'and as could be expected we were on that night. They nearly
always put you on straight from leave, get you back into the groove
as soon as possible.' No. 76 Squadron detailed twenty-four aircraft,
although one failed to take off and two came home early. Ferris
recounted his experience:

Take off at 2210 in A Apple, not our own kite as it had been

crash landed whilst we had been away, so had to go to
Hamburg in Sgt Myers' kite. This was the first raid that
Window was dropped by us. Window was the name given
to the bundles of metal strips we dropped. The bundles broke
up in the air and the metal strips just floated gently down to
earth, each strip giving a reflection on the German radar
screens. He had so many blips on the screens he didn't know
which to plot. There was a very large concentration of search
lights operating in large cones over the target, and as the
Window dropped it was not long before the search lights were
wandering about the sky anywhere. It was an amazing sight to
see those concentrated cones of lights broken up and see them
staggering about the sky. The target was well hit, 2,300 tons
of bombs dropped in 50 minutes.

One No. 76 Squadron crew failed to return that night. Sergeant
Bjercke, RNAF, and one other member of his crew were killed and the
rest captured. The next day ops were on again. Ferris remembered:

Just to break the monotony of Hamburg, they sent us to
Remscheid in the Ruhr, again a heavy concentration of search
lights, but the flak was moderate. Saw two Halifaxes shot
down in flames. A cone of search lights to port with a Halifax
in and a cone to the starboard with one in. That left the way
clear for us to go through (it's an ill wind) over the target. As
we went through the aircraft on the port side was hit by flak
and went on fire, the other was going down with smoke and
flames coming away from the two port engines and a German
fighter following it down. We saw three parachutes open up
but no more. It's rather unnerving to see your own kites being
shot down. Everyone in A Apple was very quiet. Again we
managed to get through without a scratch. Flying time for the
trip was 5 hours 40 minutes.

Fifteen aircraft were lost on the Remscheid raid. There was a total loss of life on the No. 76 Squadron crew of Sergeant Cole. Ops were on again on 2 August. Ferris recalled, 'No need to say where we went the next time, good old Hamburg.'

[Ferris:] This raid was not so good as the weather experts were wrong in their calculations. The electrical storm which was supposed to be over France was in fact over Hamburg and district. As we approached Hamburg we started to feel the effect of the storm. Blue sparks running up and down the guns, a blue haze across the windscreens making your eyes hurt when you tried to look out. Large blue streaks of lightning coming off the prop blades and the kite bucking like a bronco.

[George:] We ran into a severe electrical storm with heavy icing and although being heated the pitot head (positioned under the wing and through which the air travels to control the airspeed indicator) iced up and I had to judge my speed using engine revs and the rate and climb indicator.

[Ferris:] George decided to try and climb above it, but it didn't get any better as we didn't seem to be able to get over the top of it. We still kept on with conditions getting worse as we flew further into the storm. I just hung on with both hands, and hoped for the best, I had to hang on to the kite as it was being tossed about like a cork on the sea. God I was scared. I thought why the heck doesn't George give the order to jettison and let's get out of here. With this load of bombs and we get struck by lightning we shouldn't know much about it. If I'd been told to go down the kite for something I don't think I could have moved. I felt frozen to the spot. George must have been having quite a struggle with the controls, trying to keep her more or less straight and level.

Bomber Command pilot George Dunn DFC L d'H *(George Dunn)*

George (first right in the picture with the dog, and second right in the picture with the helmets) with LDV 'Home Guard' colleagues John Castle, 'Chummy' Nutten, and Roy Olive. *(George Dunn)*

From left to right, George with friends Cyril Purrot and John Castle, 1943. *(George Dunn)*

No. 20 OTU Lossiemouth 1942. Left to right, Dixie Dean, Reg McCadden, George, Jock Todd, Andy Maitland. *(George Dunn)*

George Dunn, centre, with his No. 76 Squadron crew in August 1943. Left to right are Reg McCadden, navigator, 'Dixie' Dean, rear gunner, 'Jock' Todd, wireless operator/air gunner, George Dunn, pilot, Ferris Newton, flight engineer, Andy Maitland, bomb aimer, Arthur (Joe) Scrivener, mid upper gunner. *(George Dunn)*

RAF Holme-on-Spalding Moor, No. 76 Squadron. George to the left of the front group. Right of George is the 'colonel' intelligence officer Squadron Leader Ivor Jones. To his left is Station Commander Group Captain Hodson, 1943. *(George Dunn)*

George with 'George' the flight commander's dog, at RAF Wyton, No. 1409 Flight, 1945. *(George Dunn)*

Clive Bancroft and George sitting on the tail of a Mosquito, No. 1409 Met Flight, RAF Wyton, early 1945. *(George Dunn)*

No. 1409 (Meteorological) Flight Mosquito PR Mk IX. November 1944. *(George Dunn)*

VE-Day 1945 outside the Officer's Mess at RAF Wyton. George with pint glass at waist level to the left of centre. Dummies of Mussolini, Hitler, and Hirohito hang above. To the right is Air Vice Marshal Donald Bennett, CB, CBE, DSO, and Russian officers. *(George Dunn)*

No. 10 SQUADRON. MELBOURNE, YORKS.

YEAR 1943		AIRCRAFT		PILOT, OR 1ST PILOT	2ND PILOT, PUPIL OR PASSENGER	DUTY (INCLUDING RESULTS AND REMARKS)
MONTH	DATE	Type	No.			
						TOTALS BROUGHT FORWARD
APRIL	3rd	HALIFAX	DT791	P/O HELLIS	SELF	OPERATIONS - ESSEN
APRIL	4th	HALIFAX	HR669	P/O HELLIS	SELF	OPERATIONS - KIEL

No. 1663 CONVERSION UNIT, RUFFORTH, YORKS.

		MK.5.				
APRIL	13th	HALIFAX	'F'	F/LT. WOODHATCH	SELF	CONVERSION. EX. 1.
"	"	"	"	"	SGT. EBELING	PASSENGER.
"	"	"	"	P/O BISSETT	"	"
"	14th	"	'B'	"	"	AIR TEST.
"	14th	"	B.	F/LT. WOODHATCH	"	CONVERSION. EX. 2.
"	"	"	'B'	"	SGT. EBELING	PASSENGER.
"	15th	"	'C'	P/O BISSETT	"	"
"	"	"	"	SELF	CONVERSION. EX. 2:3
"	"	"	"	SELF	SGT. EBELING	" CIRCUITS & LANDING
"	15th	"	B	P/O BISSETT	SELF	" " "
"	"	"	C'	"	SGT. EBELING	PASSENGER.
"	16th	"	B	F/LT. WOODHATCH	"	"
"	17th	"	A'	" "	SELF	CHECK
"	"	"	A'	SELF	SGT. EBELING EX.5 CIRCUITS. LANDINGS
"	18th	"	B'	F/LT. WOODHATCH	SELF	CHECK
"	"	"	'B'	SELF	SGT. EBELING	EX 5
"	18th	"	B	F/LT. WOODHATCH	"	PASSENGER
"	"	"	B'	SGT. EBELING	SELF	2nd PILOT

GRAND TOTAL [Cols. (1) to (10)]
379 Hrs. 35 Mins.   TOTALS CARRIED FORWARD

George's logbook showing his first operational sorties. *(George Dunn)*

YEAR 1943		AIRCRAFT		PILOT, OR 1ST PILOT	2ND PILOT, PUPIL OR PASSENGER	DUTY (INCLUDING RESULTS AND REMARKS)
MONTH	DATE	Type	No.			
—	—	—	—	—	—	— TOTALS BROUGHT FORWARD
July	11th	MK.IA. HALIFAX	H	SELF	CREW	CONSUMPTION TEST &
				W/O. SGT ELSEY F/S	R-JONES.	AIR FIRING.
-	12th	"	G	SELF	CREW	FIGHTER AFFILIATION
					F/S R JONES	& AIR TEST
-	13th	"	G	SELF	CREW	OPS. AACHEN. 8/10 cloud
				2ND PILOT	F/S R-JONES.	Flak weak - no s/Ls.
						Accurate results not observed
-		-	G	SELF	CREW	S.B.A. PRACTICE (CANCELLED)
-	15th	"	G	SELF	CREW	OPS. MONTGELIARD. Few
				2ND PILOT.	F/S. R-JONES	defences. Good photo & astro fixes
-	20th	-	G	SELF	CREW	AIR FIRING & AIR TEST
		G	WRITTEN OFF WHILST	ON LEAVE.		
-	29th	-	'A'	SELF	SGT'S MAITLAND - TODD	AIR TEST 2 circuits
					NEWTON - DEAN.	& LANDINGS.
-	29th	-	'A'	SELF	CREW.	OPS. HAMBURG. Numerous
				NAV.	SGT. PARTRIDGE	s/Ls Flak moderate. Good prang.
-	30th	"	'A'	SELF	CREW.	OPS. REMSCHEID. (Ruhr)
				NAV.	SGT. PARTRIDGE	Clear weather - Target
				2ND PILOT	F/O NOURSE	defences weak - Very good
						results. Saw 4 shot down.
			SUMMARY FOR JULY 1943		1. HALIFAX.	
			UNIT: 76 Sqd. HOLME		A/c	
			DATE. 1st AUGUST.		TYPES.	
			SIGNATURE	G.A.Dunn		

GRAND TOTAL [Cols. (1) to (10)]
563 Hrs. 05 Mins.

TOTALS CARRIED FORWARD

George's logbook, July 1943. *(George Dunn)*

YEAR 1943		AIRCRAFT		PILOT, OR 1ST PILOT	2ND PILOT, PUPIL OR PASSENGER	DUTY (INCLUDING RESULTS AND REMARKS)
MONTH	DATE	Type	No.			
				—	—	TOTALS BROUGHT FORWARD
AUGUST	6th	MK.6 HALIFAX	A	SELF	USUAL CREW	OPS. HAMBURG.
					2nd PILOT SGT. ROBERSON	Encountered Severe electrical
						storm. Heavy icing & severe
						static conditions. Jettisoned
						Bombs 1hr before E.T.A
"	7th	"	B	SELF	CREW (LESS NAV)	AIR FIRING - HORNSEA
"	9th	"	A	SELF	CREW	OPS. MANNHEIM Good
						Trip. Defences ineffective
"	12th	"	F	SELF	CREW (LESS NAV) & R/O. F/O REYNOLDS.	AIR TEST
"	12th	"	B	SELF	CREW	OPS. MILAN Uneventful
					R/G. SGT. SCOTT	trip. Defences weak. Over
					2nd PILOT F/O REYNOLDS	the Alps in moonlight!!
"	15th	"	D	SELF	CREW (LESS R/G & NAV)	AIR TEST.
"	16th	"	G	SELF	CREW (LESS R/G)	FUEL CONSUMPTION TEST
						AIR FIRING, AIR TEST (NIGHT & DAY)
"	17th	"	G	SELF	CREW	OPS. PEENEMÜNDE
					R/G SGT. WEAVER	Brilliant Moonlight - Good
					2nd PILOT SGT. MATTHEWS	Trip. Diverted to Wymeswold.
"	18th	"	Z	FL/LT. HODSON	SELF & CREW	Secret Research Station WYMESWOLD TO BASE.
"	22nd	"	G	SELF	CREW (LESS NAV)	AIR TEST.
"	22nd	"	G	SELF	CREW	OPS. LEVERKUSEN. 10/10 cloud
						Intense flak. No S/Es. P.F.F. 1/10

GRAND TOTAL [Cols. (1) to (10)]
602 Hrs. **05** Mins.

TOTALS CARRIED FORWARD

George's logbook, August 1943. *(George Dunn)*

NO. 608 SQUADRON DOWNHAM MARKET NORFOLK

YEAR 1945		AIRCRAFT		PILOT, OR 1ST PILOT	2ND PILOT, PUPIL OR PASSENGER	DUTY (INCLUDING RESULTS AND REMARKS)
MONTH	DATE	Type	No.			
						TOTALS BROUGHT FORWARD
MARCH	1st	MOSQUITO MkXX H	KB347	SELF	P/O BANCROFT	N.F.T
-- --	1st	-- --	KB347	SELF	P/O BANCROFT	OPS: BERLIN (☆) 4x500lb FLAK HIT ON SPINNERS
-- --	3rd	-- --	KB347	SELF	P/O BANCROFT	N.F.T. BOMBING AT WHITTLESEA
-- --	3rd	-- --	KB358	SELF	P/O BANCROFT	OPS: BERLIN (4) 4x500lb
-- --	5th	-- -- G	KB358	SELF	P/O BANCROFT	N.F.T.
-- --	6th	-- --	KB355	SELF	P/O BANCROFT	OPS: BERLIN (☆) DIVERTED TO L. STAUGHTON 4x500lb
-- --	6th	-- -- B	KB355	SELF	P/O BANCROFT	LITTLE STAUGHTON TO BASE
-- --	7th	-- --	KB446	SELF	P/O BANCROFT	OPS: BERLIN (☆) 3x500lb 1x500lb
-- --	8th	-- --	KB358	SELF	P/O BANCROFT	OPS: BERLIN (☆) 3x500lb 1x500lb
-- --	9th	OXFORD X	V3517	F/LT BARTHOLOMEW	P/O McCARTNEY	BASE TO BOURNE
-- --	9th	MOSQUITO	KB493	SELF	P/O McCARTNEY	BOURNE TO BASE
-- --	10th	-- --	KB356	SELF	P/O BANCROFT	N.F.T. LOW CIRCUITS
-- --	10th	-- -- O	KB356	SELF	P/O BANCROFT	OPS: BERLIN (☆) 3x500lb 1x500lb
-- --	12th	-- --	KB355	SELF	P/O BANCROFT	N.F.T
-- --	12th	-- -- B	KB355	SELF	P/O BANCROFT	OPS: BERLIN (☆) 3x500lb 2x500lb
-- --	13th	XXV	KB356	SELF	P/O BANCROFT	N.F.T.
-- --	13th	XXV	KB356	SELF	P/O BANCROFT	OPS: BERLIN (☆) 3x500lb 1x500lb
-- --	15th	XX	KB355	SELF	P/O BANCROFT	N.F.T.
-- --	15th		KB355	SELF	P/O BANCROFT	OPS: ERFURT 3x500lb 3 FLARES
-- --	16th	XXV	KB356	SELF F/LT LONG		BASE TO WOODBRIDGE
-- --	16th	XX	KB493	SELF		WOODBRIDGE TO BASE
-- --	17th		KB355	SELF	P/O BANCROFT	N.F.T.
-- --	17th	B	KB355	SELF	P/O BANCROFT	OPS: BERLIN (☆) 3x500lb 1x500lb
-- --	18th	OXFORD	V3517	W/C ALABASTER	SELF P/O BANCROFT	BASE TO BARFORD

GRAND TOTAL [Cols. (1) to (10)]
1196 Hrs 20 Mins.

TOTALS CARRIED FORWARD

YEAR 1945		AIRCRAFT		PILOT, OR 1ST PILOT	2ND PILOT, PUPIL OR PASSENGER	DUTY (INCLUDING RESULTS AND REMARKS)
MONTH	DATE	Type	No.			
						TOTALS BROUGHT FORWARD
APRIL	8	MK XVI MOSQUITO	"A" 786	SELF	F/O BANCROFT	CARNABY TO BASE
	9	—	"A" 786	SELF	F/LT ADAMS	PRE-MET RECCE. ? SNOOPER ON VHF MET TO MB KIEL (42) CINE CAMERA USED BASE - READING - SELSEY
	11	MK IX MOSQUITO	"D" ML897	SELF	F/O BANCROFT	PAMPA(3) CHERBOURG - LORIENT - BASE
	12	OXFORD	H280	SELF	F/O BANCROFT F/LT ADAMS	TO DOWNHAM MARKET & RETURN BASE - BRIDPORT
	12	MK XVI MOSQUITO	"B" 736	SELF	F/O BANCROFT	PAMPA STOOGE(1) 4800 0700W BASE
	14	—	"F" 734	SELF	F/O BANCROFT	PAMPA(4) BASE-WELLS-STODD-STETTIN OPS(43) CELLE-DAN-HEYDER-BASE
	15	—	"Cr" 737	SELF	A.C. HODGE	AIR TEST.
	16	—	"C" 733	SELF	F/O BANCROFT	PAMPA(5) BASE-WELLS-DR-BREMEN. OPS (44) DR-CUXHAVEN-DR-MEARS.
	20	OXFORD	H280	SELF	F/O BANCROFT F/LT ADAMS	TO HOOTON PARK & RETURN.
	26	MK XVI MOSQUITO	"C" 733	SELF	F/O BANCROFT	AIR TEST & LOW FLYING.
				SUMMARY FOR APRIL 1945	A/C ∵ MOSQUITO. MK IX. XVI	
				UNIT 1409 FLT	T 3 OXFORD	
				DATE 1ST MAY 1945	T/P	
				SIGNED 8/	SIGNATURE:	E 3
						S. 4
			1409 FLIGHT			
MAY	11	MK XVI MOSQUITO	"B" 736	SELF	F/O BANCROFT	PAMPA (6) BASE - I.O. WIGHT RIBADEO (SPAIN) 5000N 1000W - BASE
	14	—	"A" 786	SELF	F/O BANCROFT	PAMPA (7) BASE - BRIDPORT - BREST 5740 0740W - ST.GEORGES HEAD - BASE ST.VITH KAISER-
	25	—	"J" 337	SELF	F/O BANCROFT F/SGT. MACDONALD	COOKS TOUR (1) LAUTEN, KARLSRUHE LUDWIGSHAVEN MANNHEIM-DARMSTADT
	28	—	"A" 786	SELF	SELF	HANNAU, FRANKFURT, KOBLENZ, COLOGNE AACHEN
	28	—	"A" 786	SELF	F/O BANCROFT	PAMPA (8) BASE - READING - BAYEUX RUFFEC - ST.BRIEUC - STRETTIN BERLIN
	29	MK IX	"D" 897	SELF	F/O BANCROFT F/O SOUTHALL	DOWNHAM MARKET & RETURN.

GRAND TOTAL [Cols. (1) to (10)]   1248 Hrs.   25 Mins.   TOTALS CARRIED FORWARD

George's logbook, April and May 1945. *(George Dunn)*

Ferris Newton with his second wife Dorothy in the 1970s. *(Caroline Bolton)*

George with Bomber Command veteran friends Dave Fellowes L d'H and Jo Lancaster DFC at a Fighting High book signing, Duxford. *(Steve Darlow)*

Bomber Command pilot George Dunn DFC L d'H. *(Steve Darlow)*

As part of the fund raising for the Bomber Command Memorial in The Green Park, London, a veteran seven-man crew was assembled. From left to right John Banfield (wireless operator), Arthur Smith (flight engineer), Gordon Mellor (navigator), John Bell (bomb aimer), George Dunn (pilot), Harry Irons (air gunner), Dave Fellowes (air gunner). *(Steve Darlow)*

George Dunn at the Biggin Hill Heritage centre in 2019 pointing out the entry in his logbook for Spitfire Mark IX MJ 755. *(Royal Air Force Benevolent Fund)*

George gets to fly in a Spitfire for the first time in 72 years to mark Battle of Britain Day, 2019. *(Royal Air Force Benevolent Fund)*

[George:] About 14 minutes from Hamburg, the severe icing on the wing surfaces was causing the aircraft to become very unstable, the machine guns were lit up like Bunsen burners, and the tips of the props were all 'alight' with the static. It got to the stage where it would have been dangerous to go on and I reluctantly decided to jettison our bomb load and head for home.

[Ferris:] The skipper gave Andy orders to jettison and we turned on a new course for home, and I heaved a big sigh of relief. On the way back through gaps in the cloud we could see small fires burning all over the place, where other kites had jettisoned. Coming back over the sea I looked back towards Hamburg and I could still see the lightning flashes in the sky. I felt much better now, next land fall would be good old England. Flying time for the trip 5 hours 25 minutes and the worse scare I've had up to now.

[George:] A large number of aircraft made an early return that night and the following morning I was called on to the Flight Commander's office and reprimanded for, in his words, 'endangering the lives of the crew and possible loss of a valuable aircraft.' I did not agree with his assessment of the situation as I considered at all times I was in control and jettisoned as and when it became necessary. Yes, I did carry on without an ASI but by use of the other instruments I knew approximately our airspeed and I would never put my crew in danger if I had not felt confident about things. Apparently the well used RAF saying 'press on regardless' did not apply in this case.

George was not the only pilot fighting the weather that night. Of the twenty No. 76 Squadron aircraft crew that took off from RAF Holme-on-Spalding-Moor that night only seven believed that they had bombed the primary target; two others bombed alternatives.

In the squadron ORB, against the name of pilot New Zealander Flight Sergeant Dillon and crew, it was recorded that since take-off 'nothing has been heard'. The entire crew now rest in Hamburg cemetery.

In regard to the series of attacks on Hamburg, Ferris would record that 'by 3 August over five square miles of the city had been devastated. … The port was virtually wiped out in one week during which the RAF and American Army Eighth Air Force dropped more than 10,000 tons of bombs.' Ferris also noted an account from a Nazi war reporter, Dr Wieninger:

> Mountains of broken glass can be seen about the streets. Bomb craters are everywhere and wherever one turns there are burning buildings. Loud crashes from time to time denote the collapse of damaged houses. Among the buildings destroyed are the State library, the Pholia theatre, the Opera House, the city Hall, St George's Church, the Nicolai Church and St Matthew Church. All the amusement centres have gone. It is difficult yet to ascertain the losses among the population and the full extent of the damage, but they are very heavy. Standing in the Reeperbahn I saw great burning facades. Driving through the streets, through piles of glass splinters, rubble and debris, past craters with flaming timber crashing down, and barring the way, was not easy. Often enough we had to turn back. We went to the Lombard Bridge and looked across at the Alster Basin, where we saw a frightful sight. Everywhere smoke rose from where the buildings' commercial centre of town once stood. Time bombs are still exploding all over the place. Everywhere in the streets there are sticks of incendiaries. Smoke hangs over the town like a gigantic black storm cloud. There is only one thin red slice of sun. It is as dark this morning as it was at midnight.

Shortly after the Hamburg raids, on 5 August 1943, the *USS Plymouth* was attacked and sunk by *U-566*, which had been laid down at the Blohm & Voss works in Hamburg. Ninety-five lives were lost.

A week into August and the crew undertook some air/sea firing practice in Hornsea bay. It was also an opportunity, as Ferris recalled, for some low flying, 'one of the best things':

> This gives the real thrill of speed. Fields, hedges, farms, and roads all flashing past in quick succession. George had the kite well down having to lift her over hedges and trees, when we saw a farmer on a tractor in a field ahead, so we made a bee line for him. Shot over his head at the same time putting the kite into a climb. We looked back and there he was standing up on his tractor shaking his fist at us and I've no doubt swearing at us as well. Frightened him to death poor chap. Before going back to base went over Tunstall but nobody saw us.
>
> The next op was on 9 August in B Baker. Took off at 2240 bound for Mannheim. There was not much flak or search lights but quite a few 'scarecrows'. These were shot up into the air, burst into flames and fell to earth giving the impression of an aeroplane being shot down. You could be easily misled by them but in spite of the scarecrows the attack was pressed well home. Again we were routed back through France so the flying time was 6 hours 40 minutes.

The 'scarecrow' phenomenon is often reported by aircrew to this day. It does seem, however, that there is no definite evidence that the Germans had such munitions. In all likelihood, the 'scarecrows' were exploding aircraft. One No. 76 Squadron aircraft failed to return from the Mannheim raid, Australian Flight Lieutenant Shannon and his entire crew killed as a result of flak. (The same Flight Lieutenant Shannon who had previously flown George's aircraft back in from a raid to Essen in July, crash-landing the badly damaged Halifax.)

Three days after the Mannheim op, Ferris noticed that their aircraft was being fitted with long-range tanks. 'We thought Berlin maybe?' But when all was revealed in the briefing room, 'we saw the red ribbon stretched away down France and on into Italy. Target for tonight, Milan.' Bomber Command was being called upon to keep up the pressure on an Italian surrender, which indeed came about the following month. Of the raid George recalled: 'The only bonus was seeing the Alps in brilliant moonlight, a truly wonderful sight, but our flying time was our longest ever at nine hours twenty-six minutes, a long time to be sitting on one position.'

Having taken off at 20.48hrs, the wheels of George's Halifax touched down at RAF Holme-on-Spalding-Moor at 06.14 the following morning. A flight time, as Ferris recounted, 'which is long enough for anybody. I'll put the description of this raid in the much more capable hands of Mr Joe Illingworth of the *Yorkshire Post*, who was at our station on the night of this raid.'

Men Who Bombed Milan
Returning crews talk of their job and Mont Blanc
by our special correspondent J. Illingworth

The men who went to Milan had supper before they left at tables set with marigolds and wild roses. At dusk they took off. It was a flawless performance. Their big four engine bombers roared down the runway at intervals of one every minute. You could not pack them closer than that without tangling them in each other's slip streams.

In the control room it was a mathematical problem, of symbols and signs chalked up on blackboards; of short sharp telephone conversations, of check and countercheck. To the people on the balcony of the control room, on the roof, on the grass verge below, and at the far end of the runway where they were a smudge in the fading light, it was a human problem. As each bomber roared by and became airborne, all eyes strained to catch its distinguishing letter of the alphabet.

K for Kittie roared past and lifted her great wings to the sky, and the Canadian rear gunner who had been standing tensely on the roof of the control tower suddenly punched out his fist and raised his thumb. He stood thus, rigidly for a moment, and then he dropped his arm and relaxed, and muttered his prayer.

Night after night the bombers go out, and all those who are left behind on the station come to watch them go. It is a custom which is as old as the war itself, and yet is new each night and is always moving. The Group Captain stood on the balcony with his glasses trained on the take-off. [Those who had served] soup and the poached eggs to the crews of the bombers an hour or so before now stood watching solemnly from the roof of an air raid shelter.

When the bombers came back it was not yet light. They had 'stooged' along as they came through eight or nine hours of darkness, to Italy and back, a journey of 1,700 miles, and had delivered up their crews. Now the waitresses who had stood on the air raid shelter were moving and smiling about the tables with more poached eggs and racks filled with hot toast.

There was conversation at the tables. About Milan now left blazing behind them? No, not about Milan. About Mont Blanc, their tired eyes lit up as they spoke about Mont Blanc, lovely in her cap of snow under the light of a three-quarter moon, with great Alpine ranges spread about her. 'I've seen something I'd have paid a few pounds to see in peace-time,' says a rear gunner with sudden gusto. 'Those Alps looked wizard.'

Another rear gunner uses almost the same words. 'The Alps by moonlight,' he says with slow delight as though quoting the tourist posters. 'That would have cost me a lot of money in civvie street.'

It was about Mont Blanc that they talked first when they came in to make their reports to the Intelligence Officers. An Australian said confidentially, 'The old Alps were worth the trip.' It seems that the entire crew of his bomber had burst

into excited chatter about the great snowy ranges as they
sailed inexorably forward and over. 'If only I had a camera.'
'What a wizard photograph by moonlight, if you could get it.'

At the bar in the Mess before take-off an officer finished his
soft drink in sudden haste. 'See you tomorrow,' he said to the
barman. The barman smiled and called after him, 'The very
best, sir.' It was a warm bright smile touched with anxiety.

Some of the crews whistled shrilly or sang snatches of
popular songs as they collected their gear. Outside the hut
the navigators were squatting on their packs, entering the
latest weather information on their charts. 'Coo,' said one a
little aghast. 'There are fourteen different sets of wind. Have
you heard?'

The lorries came up to take them out to the aircraft at
their dispersal points. I went out to one of them. The crew
of the aircraft were standing about smoking a last cigarette.
I remembered what the Wing Commander had said, 'The
only trying time is when you have been briefed, and you know
you are on, and you are scratching about getting a meal and
having a last cigarette. Once you get your engine you are
all right.'

The great black planes crawled out and came onto the
run-way, and then they had got their engines and they were
all right.

Nine hours later we were hearing about Mont Blanc and
Milan. One of the men said as he drank a pint of hot tea,
'When we crossed the French coast we saw a fighter come in
and attack a Halifax. We saw the Halifax give one burst with
its rear guns and then the fighter went down in flames. We
saw it hit the ground, just after that we saw another fighter
attack a Halifax and set its outer starboard engine on fire.
The Halifax turned and we did not see it again. (This second
Halifax landed safely at an English base, its rear gunner

wounded in the foot.) Other planes reported an uneventful journey. The skipper of a plane which went into Milan on the first wave said, 'The opposition was very slight. Search lights were waving about drunkenly. I don't know what they were supposed to be doing. There was a certain amount of flak to start with, but it did not appear to be near anybody, and it was negligible when we left. We don't get anything as simple as this over Germany. Even when we left there were fires going and remember we were one of the first to bomb.'

The rear gunner of this plane said, 'When we were leaving there was a very high column of smoke over the target. As I looked back I could not see the fires for the smoke and there were occasional explosions. Opposition very poor. It looked better away over Turin.'

A pilot came in carrying ... the mascot of the aircraft. [A doll, and Ferris recalls that this was George, although actually Joe the mid-upper gunner was carrying it.] Written on the ... white waistcoat were the names of all the targets it had been taken over. 'We went in with the second wave,' said the pilot. 'We saw scattered fires as we bombed. There were explosions and they lit up the streets and picked out the outlines. As we came away and crossed the Alps we could see the fires going down well. There was a tremendous cloud in the sky at about 18,000 feet and the whole of the base was lit with the glow of the fires.'

The crew of another plane said, 'There were three major fires covering a large area. We could not really count the other fires. They were spreading all over the place. They seemed to be out of control, and we could see the streets in the centre of Milan in the glow. Our rear gunner was still talking about the fires when we were fifty miles away.'

The others I spoke to all said the flak was negligible, and that the search lights wandered 'aimlessly' about. And they all talked about Mont Blanc and the moon and how lovely it was.

Ferris added:

> There was a postscript to the Milan story. One of the kites on
> the squadron had trouble with the oxygen system, so he couldn't
> climb back over the Alps, so they went on to North Africa.
> He came back to base two or three days later loaded down
> with all kinds of things. The pilot's father was actually on the
> camp seeing the CO (as of course the crew had been reported
> missing) when their kite came to land. Quite a happy reunion.

Ferris was referring to the crew of Lieutenant Hulthin. The No. 76
Squadron Halifax of Pilot Officer McCann failed to return, the captain and four of his crew killed, and two became prisoners of war.

On 16 August Ferris recalled: 'Took over our new G for George.
Took her on a fuel consumption test, over Tunstall and the low
flying area. Had a few minutes hedge hopping.' The next day the crew
prepared for one of the most significant raids of the entire war.

Chapter Five

Hydra

On the morning of 17 August 1943 George found himself detailed for ops that night, a raid that he would later recognise as 'the most important of the whole tour', Operation Hydra. No. 76 Squadron would be contributing 22 Halifaxes to the total of 596 aircraft that would take off to attack the German secret weapon research station at Peenemünde on the Baltic Coast. A small force of Mosquitoes would also be carrying out a diversionary raid against Berlin.

Ferris noted that this was 'a bad day for the Germans. Butch Harris … had decided to send a large force of his slaves to bomb the secret weapon base at Peenemünde … on the Baltic coast. It was a big job for the pathfinder force, they had to make three aiming points all at different times.'

> [George:] When we got into the briefing room and they drew the curtains back we saw this ribbon go right up the North Sea and across Denmark. Peenemünde? Where's that? What's that all about? We'd never heard of it. We were just told it was a research station and they mentioned important radar. We weren't told it was experimental rockets. At the end of the briefing they said, 'If you don't do the job tonight, you'll go

back tomorrow night, the night after that, and the night after that', which really hit us. You can imagine the reception we would have had on the second night if we had gone back again.

[Ferris:] We were told at briefing by the AOC Group that this target must be wiped out the first time. If it was not then we should go until it was.

[George:] We were routed up the North Sea and across southern Denmark to avoid heavy flak on the north German coast and we bombed from 7,000 feet, which was about 11,000 below our usual bombing height. Originally our group, No. 4 Group, were scheduled to go in as part of the last wave.

However, a change of wind direction had presented the possibility that smoke would shield the respective aiming point for George's group. As such George found himself over the target as part of the first wave of attack, 'and it turned out that we were very lucky'.

[Ferris:] Our aiming point was on the staff blocks and living quarters for the professors. There was a lot of experimental work being carried out that we wanted to stop if we could. ...
    It was a beautiful night, with a very bright moon and the target was not actually very well defended with flak. But when Jerrie [sic] found out where the raid was actually taking place he sent up a host of night fighters. We bombed from 7,000 feet, almost low level for us chaps and we were in the first wave in, so we were clear of the target when most of the Jerrie fighters appeared. ... Crews going in in the later waves said the sky was full of fighters. Nothing like being first there, catch 'em when they are asleep.

[George:] Our aiming point was the living quarters of the scientists and technicians, and these could be clearly seen by the bomb-aimer as it was a brilliant moonlit night and the target had been well marked by the pathfinders. As far as we were concerned it was a piece of cake. The flak was only light to start with. We went in, bombed and out straight away. By the time the later waves reached the target the German night fighters, realising the attack on Berlin by Mosquitos was a diversion, arrived. Our good fortune in going in first was sadly not so for the later waves.

The last wave did indeed suffer, contributing significantly to the total of forty Bomber Command aircraft lost that night. No. 76 Squadron aircraft had all returned safely to the UK. Assessment of the raid, and the scale of destruction and disruption, gave optimism, and an immediate follow-up raid was not required. Indeed, the Peenemünde raid seriously delayed German V-weapon developments, killing key scientists and *The Bomber Command War Diaries* record 'the estimate has appeared in many sources that this raid set back the V-2 experimental programme by at least 2 months and reduced the scale of the eventual rocket attack'.

George had been forced to land away from base on return from the attack on Peenemünde. 'On the return leg it was discovered that we had a bad hydraulic leak and were instructed to land at Wymeswold.'

[Ferris:] What a bind. At Wymeswold we were given a meal, had it with their crews, who were just setting off for a daylight (in Bostons). We couldn't take off until they were all clear. Even after they had all gone they wouldn't let us away. Everyone was getting browned off as it was early lunch time. Joe, our mid-upper, sent the pigeon off back to base with the following message on its leg, 'Bogged down here with bullshit.' They were not at all pleased with him at Holme.

[George:] We had to leave our aircraft at Wymeswold and they sent a plane down from Holme to take us back. We had

to make another visit to the CO and were given a reminder
that pigeons were for emergency use only.

[Ferris:] We hadn't to go to Peenemünde the next night, the
powers that be must have been satisfied with our first attempt.

On 22nd August George's crew was detailed for a raid to Leverkusen.
Early on the day George took their Halifax for an air test, some
local flying around Hornsea and Tunstall. Unusually they would
have an extra passenger. Ferris recalled, 'On the way out to the kite
Joe said he had a passenger to go with us.'

[George:] Thinking it was a member of the ground crew
I agreed.

[Ferris:] When we got out to the kite we found Cecile, a
WAAF Officer, was the passenger.

[George:] And a very good friend of the squadron commander.
I said to Joe that this wasn't on as it would land me in trouble.
'She won't say anything,' he said, 'and in any case she is here
now.' So I reluctantly agreed. The following day I was up
before the CO, which was not very good because I had only
just been commissioned.

[Ferris:] Needless to say poor old George got a strip torn off
for taking her up. First day he was commissioned, a good start
for him.

[George:] I obviously had no excuse for my actions and kept
Joe out of the picture but I had a feeling that the CO knew
who was behind it as Joe was a wide boy and known on the
squadron as 'the fixer'. I was warned as to my future conduct
and reminded of my responsibilities as an officer. The rest of

the crew knew that Joe was behind it and gave him a rollocking for putting me in that position.

In between the air test with the unauthorised passenger and George's reprimand, there was the trip, without Cecile, to a fiercely defended German target, Leverkusen. Ferris recalled: 'There was heavy flak and ten tenths cloud. Weather man off course again, so the bombs were all over the place. Time for the trip 5 hours. The next night we were on again, long range tanks fitted as well. We were right this time – Berlin – couldn't always be Italian targets.' Andy Maitland took up the story:

> It was at the early evening briefing we were to find out that at 2000 hours that night we would be on our way to the 'Big City', Berlin. We had never been there before but we had heard many very frightening stories about the strength of the city defences. I suppose I should have felt afraid but did not seem to feel so. Perhaps this was because we had already faced the fury of Essen, Cologne, Hamburg, and all the shells the Ruhr gunners could pump into the night sky. My own view was that Berlin would have to resemble hell if their defence were to be more concentrated than those experienced in and around the city of Essen.
>
> One thing that did worry me was that the round flight would take about eight hours and quite a number of hours would be spent over German territory where their night fighter force would have plenty of time to track us down.

Andy's fears were well founded. Bomber Command would send 727 aircraft to the German capital on the night of 23/24 August 1943, of which 56 failed to return, the Command's highest loss in one night of the war to date. Ferris recounted:

> This was our first raid on Berlin. We have heard such stories

about the place – we are not at all happy about going there.
I remember every one sitting around, out at the kite, waiting
for start-up time, and nobody hardly speaking a word.
We are first wave in. Berlin is dotted with light – it is hard to
distinguish the burst of anti-aircraft shells from the coloured
markers dropped by the Pathfinders.

The first thing we have to do is fly through a wall of searchlights – hundreds, in cones and in clusters. A wall of light with
very few breaks, and behind that wall an even fiercer light –
glowing red and green and blue. Over that there are myriads
of flares hanging in the sky. There is flak coming up at us now.
All we see is a quick red glow from the ground and then up it
comes on a level – a blinding flash. It's pretty obvious as we
come in through the searchlight cones that it's going to be hell
over the target.

There is one comfort and it's been a comfort to me all the
time we have been going over – it is quite soundless. The roar
of your engines drowns everything else. It's like running
straight into the most gigantic display of soundless fireworks
in the world. We are due over the target at 23.59; that's in
about three minutes, and the bomb-aimer is lying prone over
his bomb sight, and the searchlights are coming nearer all the
time. One cone splits and then it comes together again. They
seem to splay out then stop, then come together again, and as
they do there is a Lanc right in the centre. It's getting too hot
with those searchlights, so we start weaving. George puts the
nose down and we are pelting away at a furious rate. As we are
coming out of the searchlights more flak is coming up from
the inner defence.

'Hullo Skipper.'
'Hullo Navigator.'
'Half a minute to go.'
'OK. Thanks for reminding me.'
'Keep weaving George, there is quite a lot of light stuff

coming up as well – falling off a bit low.'

'Hullo Engineer. Will you put the revs up.'

'Engineer to Pilot. Revs up Skipper.'

'OK. Keep weaving George, a lot of searchlights and fighter flares, left.'

'Hullo Bomb Aimer. OK. Bomb doors open.'

'OK George – right – steady – a little bit longer yet OK – steady – right a little bit – right – steady – bombs still going – OK bombs gone. Keep weaving, there is some flak coming up. I can actually see ground detail skipper. Oh it's a wizard sight.'

'OK Andy. Don't get excited – keep your eyes open.'

'Engineer to Pilot. Jerry fighter just passed over the top of us – port to starboard.'

'OK Engineer. Keep your eyes open gunners.'

'Hullo Skipper. Will you turn onto zero 81.'

'Zero 81 right Navigator.'

'Engineer to Pilot. Another fighter crossing our course port to starboard.'

'OK Engineer.'

'There is a master searchlight probing for us George – keep weaving.'

Its beam swings past us, down goes the nose of the aircraft, the wings dip and we feel ourselves being flung about. We are swinging away, that master light is getting further and further away. We are out of it and now we are through I turn and get a glimpse of that furious glowing carpet of light and explosions – that's all I can see of Berlin. We are beating out of it for home. The gunner's last sight of it is a great glow in the sky and around that glow a ring of searchlights, and all that's fifty miles away. We have only about another six hundred to do, but that last six hundred is covered in a much better spirit than the outward journey for everyone is light-hearted again. As we approach England we get a diversion message to proceed to Catfoss, of all things. Flying time for the trip

8 hours 5 minutes. … Two aircraft collided on the circuit at
Catfoss. Damned hard luck that, all way to Berlin and back,
then get it on your own circuit.

The aircraft lost in the collision mentioned by Ferris are likely to
be two No. 78 Squadron Halifaxes that had been directed to land
at RAF Leconfield. Fourteen lives were lost, the survivor being
seriously injured.

A welcome break from operational duties followed, the raid to
Berlin being George's twenty-fifth op. On 6 September the Dunn
crew was one of twenty detailed by No. 76 Squadron for a raid on
Munich. Ferris recalled: 'We carried a very heavy load of incendiaries on that trip. So we left a large number of fires burning. As we
came in over the Channel I told George we were getting short of
petrol. I suggested we put down and had a fill-up. We landed at
Hartford Bridge, and found some of the other crew here for the
same reason. Flying time 8 hours 35 minutes.' No. 76 Squadron New
Zealander Flight Sergeant Little failed to return from the raid, losing
his life along with five others from his crew of eight.

   Prior to their next raid, during an air test, George took his crew
over Tunstall, and received a greeting from Cath's parents. 'This
time they saw us. Pa came out with what looked like a table cloth,
and was stood in the middle of the road waving it like mad. Mother
stood at the garden gate waving.'

   For the raid on 15 September 1943 Ferris noted, 'This one was
the kind everyone wanted to go [on], including Wingco Smith. It
was a French tyre factory near Montluçon … no defences, nothing
… It was a good prang.' Pilot Officer George Dunn would be flying
with a crew of eight that night, once more accompanied by a second
dickie. It was a feature of many of George's ops, perhaps indicative
of his abilities and the confidence of his seniors. Having noted how
easy the Montluçon raid was, Ferris commented that the 'next night
they gave us a stiffer one'.

Had to bomb Modane railway station, which was at the entrance to the Mt Cenis tunnel. This raid would (the powers that be said) block up the entrance to the tunnel and so stop reinforcements going from France to Italy and so help our Army fighting up the leg of Italy.

There was only one snag on this raid and that was our old friend the weather. There was a cold front stretching right across our path in the S.E. of France, but we should be able to climb over it (so they said). In any case we should not be able to go below 10,000 feet as we would be approaching the foothills of the Alps.

We took off at 1943 hours, not climbing much above 12,000 feet as there was not a great deal of opposition on the way down France. Usual flak as we crossed the enemy coast. After we had passed Orleans we started climbing again, and by the time we were at Lyon we were in the middle of the front (of bad weather) so we started to try and climb over it. Up we went through the cloud, and things getting a little on the bumpy side, also the aircraft starting to get ice on the wings, etc. Could hear pieces of ice hitting the fuselage as they were flung off the prop blades. I changed over to the hot-air intakes to stop the carburettors from freezing up. It also boosts up your petrol consumption quite a lot. We were still climbing and bumping about, our height now about 16,000 feet and still no clear sky.

Kept looking out at the leading edges to see how much ice there was but of course couldn't hardly see a thing. One's thoughts, which always work overtime on these occasions, were perhaps much worse than what our actual condition actually was.

Clear sky, George decided to press on a bit further as we were only about half an hour's flying time from the target. Plunged into still more cloud, climb, climb, but the old kite had just about reached her ceiling. I kept looking at the airspeed which was dropping and I was expecting her to stall any moment. I hoped George had his eye on it as well. Everywhere you looked seemed to have ice on it.

[George:] We were about 30 minutes from the target when the icing became very severe and pieces of ice were being felt hitting the aircraft, plus, once again, the airspeed indicator failed due to icing and on this occasion I decided that enough was enough and turned back.

[Ferris:] At last George gave the order, 'Jettison bombs, give me a new course for base Nav.' I had been watching the contents of the petrol tanks, getting lower and lower and I thought our next worry is going to be shortage of petrol. Anyway with this new order of the Skipper's I could put her back into cold air and drop the revs and boost, give her a nice slow descent for the English coast. It was my only experience of icing conditions, but once was enough for me. Even with all that ice I was still sweating like a bull. When we got back to base found out that hardly anyone got there, and we were not surprised either.

[George:] On this occasion I did not have to see the flight commander as apparently a large number of aircraft also turned back.

There is an amusing typo in the No. 76 Squadron ORB for this raid, which records a 'Summary of Attack on Mundane'. Perhaps an intentional ironic typo as clearly the raid on Modane had not been mundane. The ORB scribe also records that, 'the elements were dead against us on the outward trip. Severe icing was encountered and many were compelled to turn back.'

The date of 21 September 1943 marked George's 21st birthday. Ferris recalled, 'They made him a birthday cake and a giant key. Cecile,

the WAAF Officer we gave the unauthorised flight to, made a piece
of poetry, which goes as follows:

I feel today your 21st
You quite deserve a line
Please don't think me any worse
For keeping it in rhyme

A birthday card with roses red
With key and birds of blue
With sloppy line (you might have read)
I would have brought for you

But this I feel might not be kind
To Peggy fair and gay
To whom, I know, love all too blind
Has led your heart away

To you and crew of Johnny wolf
Shall always have a part
No matter where and how you are
Of my old fickle heart

There's Joe the changeless always gay
On intercom a treat
For him may clouds be silver lined
And Lilies always sweet

I'm sure that he 'tween cups of tea
Has whittled you a heart
Of Perspex clear with letter P
Entwined through Cupid's dart

There's Andy too, so shy and fair

Who's newly joined our throng
With big blue eyes and curly hair
He'll settle there e'er long

And Dixie now complete with crowns
A Canadian forsooth
To turret rear when G comes down
Gets water in his boots

There's Ferris too complete with car
Supplies the 'wolves' their needs
On stand down nights they travel far
To the 'Old Ball' near Leeds

Now Jock the handsome wireless op
Whose also lost his heart
It has not strayed too far from 'Holme'
In Beverley apart

G for George I wish you both
And all you merry crew
The very best of love and luck
And HAPPY LANDINGS TOO.'

On 29 September Ferris recorded: 'Came back from leave in time
to go with the boys to Bochum, third visit. Still the large concentration of search lights, but the flak was only moderate (must be
getting used to it). The target was well pranged.' The Bochum raid
was George's 29th operational sortie and for 3 October Ferris would
write: 'Our last trip. The target was Kassel with a spoof attack on
Hanover by Mosquitos, and very well it worked.' George recalls,
'For our final sortie we were naturally apprehensive about our
chances, but slightly relieved when we found that the target was
Kassel and not the Ruhr. It was an unknown quantity.' Andy

Maitland would recount: 'The tension was quite apparent on the faces of our crew as we attended the mid-afternoon briefing on 3 October, for this was to be the final operational sortie of our tour. My eyes never moved from the briefing map as the cover was removed revealing the target to be Kassel. First impression, "Well thank goodness it's not the Ruhr" and I am sure the others in the crew agreed wholeheartedly.' The German defences would, however, exact their toll that night. The No. 76 Squadron ORB entry for the raid records: 'Twenty aircraft were detailed for this attack on Kassel which had been subject to a terrific battering by the RAF on many previous occasions. Unfortunately, the Squadron suffered, numerically, one of its heaviest losses.' Indeed, 4 of the squadron's Halifaxes would fail to return, with 17 lives lost, and 12 men captured. At 18.01hrs Pilot Officer George Dunn lifted Halifax V LK903 'G' from the runway at RAF Holme-on-Spalding-Moor.

[George:] A great crowd stood on the control tower and the controller's caravan at the end of the runway to wave us off, which was most encouraging.

[Ferris:] This being our last trip we got a really marvellous send-off by everyone. A whole crowd of people on the Officers' Mess site waving like mad, then as we taxied round to take off we came past the main sites with another large crowd waving and shouting. Flying control types, Met. officer, and the Group Captain out on the balcony of the flying control tower. At the ACP caravan at the end of the runway's edges Squadron Leader Bennett, Captain Stene and others all giving the thumbs-up sign. With a send-off like that (which shook me) we couldn't help but come back.

Jerry had two lines of flares leading to Hanover, but we were going to Kassel, the sky was nice and dark over Kassel. This was a new idea of Jerries [sic], to drop a line of flares on either side of the main stream of bomber, and it made it as bright as day. Then his fighters could come in for the kill.

[George:] Despite encountering some heavy flak over the target we were grateful to get through and be heading home. I used extra revs on our run up from the south coast, determined to be first back, and we were the first to land at 35 minutes past midnight.

[Ferris:] Needless to say we were first back, the only time we were. As we touched down we all gave a loud shout through the intercom, and as George had it on transmit all and sundry heard what we said. Anyway nobody cared. I know we didn't.

[Andy Maitland:] As George braked and the aircraft came to a stop at the end of our landing run a great cheer rang out over the intercommunication system. A cheer for George who was a great pilot and a great captain; also the cheer was one of relief and great joy that we had survived a tour of operations and as I stepped from the aircraft I felt like kissing the ground.

[Ferris:] After debriefing etc, I gave Catherine a ring on the phone, just to tell her I was back and finished. That was about three o'clock in the morning. Phill [a girlfriend of Catherine's] was with her so they had a drink in bed just to celebrate.

Back at Holme we were having our second breakfast in the Officers' Mess kitchen, so we could be with the rest of the crew. There was [sic] only three of us who were not commissioned by this time.

[George:] Any euphoria that we felt was quickly dampened the following day, when the adjutant woke me up and said, 'I'm sorry but we've got rather an unpleasant task for you.' We had to escort four coffins to York station, these being the

crews of two Mosquitos which had crashed nearby, and they
were to be buried where their families came from, the
undertakers were at the station. We didn't get a lot of detail
about how they were killed. We didn't really want to know.
We had to sit in the back of a lorry with these coffins. This
made a really sombre ending to our tour.

[Ferris:] So that ended my first tour of ops. I think we had
been very lucky to come through without any trouble. The
gunners never fired a shot on any trip we were on, only hit
once by flak. Most of our targets had been in Happy Valley.
We were now rested for six months, after which you were
supposed to do another twenty.

It was now time for George to say farewell to his crew, as each
received postings to various units. 'This was quite traumatic after
having been so closely knit together for so many months, but it was
just one of those things one had to accept in service life.' Andy
Maitland commented:

I will always think myself privileged to have been a member
of George Dunn's crew, for to me this crew had everything
required to make them an efficient operational crew. They
were well disciplined, worked well together as a team while
on operations. They never shirked the task set them and often
forced home their attack against the fiercest of defences. The
camaraderie that was to be born in the heat of battle exists to
this day. All of them were brave men as all operational crew
were brave men and they all knew the survival odds [were]
stacked against them. I will always feel honoured to have been
associated with this crew and thankful that we were the lucky
ones for many thousands of equally brave and efficient aircrew whose luck ran out lay dead in the battlefields of Europe.

Chapter Six

From Mossies to Spitfires

Six weeks after completing his tour George received some awful news: 'My rear gunner Cyril "Dixie" Dean had died of Diphtheria. Dixie was a 19-year-old Canadian from Toronto and a cheerful character who made us laugh with some of his Canadian expressions, and a habit of putting jam on his kippers. I wrote to his mother as soon as I received the news and had a nice letter back.'

Cyril Armstrong 'Dixie' Dean died on 14 November 1943 and is buried in Peel Green Cemetery, on the outskirts of Manchester. The inscription on his grave reads, 'In life loved and honoured, in death remembered. Mom, Dad, Art and Doug. Toronto, Canada.' George received the news while he was at No. 18 OTU at RAF Worksop, a satellite of RAF Finningley, and from the end of November into December he completed a course at No. 93 Group Screened Pilot's School, RAF Church Broughton.

It was in December, when George went home on leave, that he received good news. He had been awarded the Distinguished Flying Cross.

I didn't know until I got home. The news was in the *Whitstable Times*. My mother said, 'Why didn't you tell us?' I had a job to tell her that I didn't know. I phoned the paper and asked the editor and he told me he had got the information from the *London Gazette*. I missed out on an investiture at Buckingham Palace. After the war finished, I wrote to the Air Ministry and said, 'Look, I had a gong in 1943. Where is it?' I got it by post.

On his return to No. 18 OTU, George accumulated flying hours as an instructor, passing on his operational experience. Even though he was away from the hostile skies on the continent, risk and danger was ever present. It is one of the sad and sobering statistics associated with Bomber Command that thousands upon thousands of airmen were killed during training. On 20 January 1944, George was in charge of night flying:

There was a bit of haze about. One of my pupils was a flying officer, they were starting to come in from Training Command to go operational. This chap, Flying Officer Jennings, was quite experienced. He was doing his night circuits and bumps, with his crew, in a Wellington. I decided to go up with him to do a weather check and make sure that it was OK for the pupils to fly. On landing and after he taxied round I arranged for a lorry to pick me up at the end of the runway so that he could go straight off. He took off, came round, and for some reason or other he did an overshoot. And that was it. Never heard any more from him. They'd crashed. It was later revealed that a prop blade had come off.

The Wellington had crashed in the grounds of Worksop College and was consumed by fire. Thirty-year-old Flying Officer Richard Jennings is buried in Southend-on-Sea (Sutton Road) Cemetery. Twenty-year-old Sergeant Patrick Downes, is buried in Great Crosby (Saints Peter and Paul) Roman Catholic Churchyard. Pilot Officer Colin Sears rests in Beckenham Cemetery. Sergeant Kenneth Sillatoe, twenty-two, is buried in Harrogate (Stonefall) Cemetery.

The body of 21-year-old Pilot Officer Robert Wade rests in Islington Cemetery.

In June 1944 George carried out an instructor's course at No. 3 Flying Instructors' School, RAF Lulsgate Bottom, Bristol, after which he returned to Finningley, soon to inscribe his 1,000th flying hour in his logbook. By December 1944, however, George had had his fill of instructional duties:

> I'd done a fair stint and it does get a bit boring, especially when you are doing circuits and bumps with pupils, and cross countries at night. I met a navigator instructor at OTU, Flying Officer Bancroft, and we got quite pally. He lived in Stretford, near Manchester, and I often spent leave with him and his family. He was short in stature so was affectionally [sic] known as Tich, a very friendly and cheerful character. One day a notice came up on daily routine for volunteers for Mosquito training. He was in the same frame of mind as me, he was getting a bit cheesed off, so I said, 'How do you fancy it?' He said, 'Yes, sure' and we put in for it.
>
> We found ourselves posted to No. 1655 Mosquito Training Unit at RAF Upper Heyford, Oxfordshire, and thence on to the satellite station at Barford St John, near Banbury. The course lasted exactly a month and had been subject to some delay because of some very severe weather during this period, a lot of our time being spent clearing snow from the runways.

When George is asked about his views on the Mosquito, 'Beautiful' is always his first response.

> When I volunteered to go back on operations on Mosquitos I knew that it was a good aircraft but did not realise that it would turn out to receive the accolades it has. When I sat in the right-hand seat for the first take-off I very quickly realised

how lucky I was to be able to fly in such a wonderful machine. It really had everything, speed, height and versatility. It was easy on the controls and had no apparent faults apart from a tendency to swing on take-off. It really was exhilarating flying this aircraft and I managed to go solo after one hour fifty minutes in daylight and fifty minutes at night. Later on in my career I flew Spitfires but will always consider the Mossie as my favourite aircraft.

George's first flight in a Mosquito was on 1 February 1945 as a second pilot to Squadron Leader Buckley, on a Mosquito Mk III, HJ853, his logbook recording 'familiarisation, taxying, stalling, steep turns, simulation of engine failure on take-off, circuits and landings'. Then on 4 February with a Flight Lieutenant Wall, in LR856, a 50-minute flight, 'overshoot flapless landing, s.e. landings (feathered and unfeathered), action in event of fire'. Shortly after, George recorded his name in the '1st pilot' column and completed 1 hour 5 minutes of circuits and landings. On 13 February he carried out a 1-hour 45-minute 'Bomber solo' in a Mark XXV, KB514. That night, a forty-minute 'night dual', and the following night after a ten-minute dual flight, George was on his own for a 1-hour 5 minute 'night solo'. For the rest of the month he was joined by his navigator, Bancroft, carrying out numerous cross-countries, including on 26 February a 'special loran exercise – Base–Bognor Regis–Cabourg–Orleans–DR Posn–Tours–Bayeaux–Bognor Regis–Base.' On 27 February George's 'Summary of Flying and Assessments' form recorded just over thirty hours at the controls of the Mosquito and his ability as 'proficient'. George also noted in his logbook, 'I hereby certify that together with my navigator I have carried out the two abandoning a/c drills on the ground whilst with this unit.' A posting to No. 608 Squadron, at RAF Downham Market in Norfolk, followed.

Seeking to capitalise on the speed and long-range capabilities of the Mosquito, Air Vice Marshal Don Bennett, who commanded the Pathfinder Force, had overseen the establishment of the Light

Night Striking Force (LNSF). In an all-Mosquito raid to Düsseldorf on the night of 23/24 February 1944 a No. 692 Squadron Mossie was the first to drop a 4,000lb bomb. The LNSF, detailed to carry out diversionary and harassing raids, expanded, including, at the start of August 1944, the addition of No. 608 Squadron. Having previously carried out maritime duties, the squadron took up LNSF duties flying from RAF Downham Market, and by the end of the war the squadron had flown 1,726 Mosquito sorties across 246 raids. Although there was no certainty, by the time George arrived at No. 608 Squadron, at the beginning of March 1945, he felt, 'the war was coming to an end and it was our task to keep the Germans on their toes'.

George went to work immediately. On 1 March, as part of a force of fifty-five Mosquitoes, George in KB347 took four 500lb bombs to Berlin, meeting some opposition, and recording 'flak hits on spinners'. Two nights later it was back to Berlin with the same bomb load, part of a force of sixty-four Mosquitoes. It was Berlin again on 5 March, diverted to RAF Little Staughton on return, as one of the No. 608 Squadron Mosquitoes had burst a tyre on landing and obstructed the runway. The Mosquito flown by Australian Flight Lieutenant MacLean, DFC, failed to return, the pilot and his navigator losing their lives. Of the eleven operational sorties George carried out with No. 608 Squadron in March 1945, all but one of them was to Berlin – on 15 March having attacked Erfurt.

The No. 608 Squadron ORB (Form 540) entry for the raid to Berlin on 8 March 1945 gives an impression of the nature of these raids:

9 Mosquitos to attack Berlin.

KB146 (B) F/O Smith, F/O Hart
KB406 (K) F/L Hobbs, F/O Dennis
KB355 (G) F/O Dunn, F/O Bancroft
KB347 (H) F/L Lilley, F/S Hossacks
KB346 (R) F/O Nunn, P/O Harris

KB413 (V) F/L McKenzie, F/O Scott
KB491 (P) F/L Morton, F/S Beavis
KB400 (U) F/O Barson, F/L Miles
KB189 (Z) F/L Lockyer, F/O Sherry

One aircraft returned early [F/O Smith] and one failed to
return [F/L Hobbs, but both men later reported 'safe']. The
remaining seven aircraft attacked primary dropping 23 x 500
M.C. + 7 x 500 M.C.L.D. between 2039 and 2044 hrs from
24/26000'. All crews but one received broadcast altering
H. hr to 2140 hrs. [This is an error in the ORB. This should
be 20.40hrs, as recorded by the individual crews.] The first lot
of mixed red and green T.I.s went down at 2036 hrs and were
followed by further lots until 2041. All the mixed red and green
T.I.s were well concentrated and formed a rough square which
was very compact. The floater T.I.s were also seen and appeared
to be slightly S. to SE of the T.I. concentration. Although
numerous cookie bursts were seen in the T.I.s there were one
or two undershoots. There was slight H/F and a few S/Ls
which were doused when bombing started.

Having completed his forty-first bombing operation on 29 March
1945, George's attention was now directed elsewhere.

When we were at Worksop there was another navigator, Eric
Adams, who was a friend of Bancroft's and he was on No. 1409
Met Flight at RAF Wyton, near Huntingdon. He got in touch
with us and said that they had a vacancy, and 'it's a nice little
flight, do you fancy coming to join us?' 'Yes sure' and we transferred there at the beginning of April. This Flight was a small
self-contained unit attached to the Pathfinders, No. 8 Group.
The duties were to investigate the weather conditions over target
areas prior to raids being carried out, then to report same
by scrambler telephone to Group HQ immediately on arrival

back to base. On some occasions we contacted the Master
Bomber of the main force prior to his arrival over the target
to decide which marking method would be most suitable.

(In January 1945 the Air Ministry issued a bulletin giving an account
of the history and role of No. 1409 Met Flight, – see appendix II.)

George arrived at No. 1409 Flight, RAF Wyton, in April 1945. 'On
our first practice "Pampa", the code name for the Met flights, we
had an engine failure way out over the North Sea and had to divert
to Carnaby near Bridlington. Fortunately the Mosquito could fly
quite well on one engine.' This flight took place on the 7th of the
month. Two days later George would be recording in his logbook,
'Kiel, 4.30 hours. Pre-Met recce & snooper on Kiel. VHF Mat to M.B
[Master Bomber]. Cine camera used.' Then a 4.35hrs Pampa on 14
April to the north of Germany, and a 3.20hrs Pampa to Bremen on
16 April, his forty-fourth and last operational sortie of the Second
World War.

    The war was now drawing to a close and a wonderful photograph
exists of George outside the mess at RAF Wyton with beer in hand
celebrating the end of hostilities on 8 May 1945. George's flying
duties remained, however, with further Pampas on 11 and 14 May.
Then on 23 May a 'Cooks Tour':

We made a few trips over Germany taking members of the
ground crew over so they could see the results of the raids,
the damage and gain some satisfaction from their contribution to the war effort. They had been involved in servicing
the aircraft and looking after the crews and the powers that
be thought it only right that they should have a trip over to
Germany and see what we had been up to. The damage was
unbelievable, I was surprised. In a Mosquito there's no real
room for a passenger so they had to lie in the bomb-aimer's
position, on their belly. I remember one poor chap being up

the front in a Mosquito, when they were taking off on a Cook's Tour; one of the prop blades came off and sliced his arm off.

Through the rest of May, June and July, George's logbook records further Pampas and Cooks Tours. 'There were still many military flights that demanded up to date weather reports. Two special occasions I was involved in were when Mr Churchill visited Potsdam in Germany and when the King and Queen visited the Channel Isles, which they ultimately had to do by ship as the weather conditions were very bad.'

Pasted into George's logbook, next to the entries for July 1945 is the following poem:

To Flying Officer George Dunn

'VIP' – I wrote it,
Not thinking much of you.
But since you would disclaim it
I still proclaim it true.

Does distance really matter –
Is that the only end?
From Aldegrove to Jurby
Is not so far, my friend.

And were you really airborne
For such a long long time –
Not much more, methinks, Sir,
Than spent upon this rhyme.

(F/O John Kennedy)

In August 1945 No. 1409 Met Flight transferred to RAF Upwood, on one occasion George being visited by his parents for an open day. When the flight was disbanded he transferred to No. 109 Squadron (Met Flight) at RAF Woodhall Spa, then a move to RAF Wickenby, and another to RAF Hemswell. George, along with his navigator, then saw a notice about crews volunteering for a posting to Malta, 'where they intended to set up a new Met Flight. We weren't happy on 109 Squadron. We were the only crew from 1409 that had joined and felt a bit like outcasts. We were sent to RAF Hornchurch, then commanded by Group Captain Douglas Bader, before going out to Malta.'

On 25 January 1946 George flew as a passenger on a Stirling, and on arrival in Malta it was a case of, 'Typical RAF': 'There were about 10 crews, nearly all flight lieutenants, and they didn't know anything about us. Group Captain said, "What are you doing here? We don't know anything about you." So they gave us a lorry and a hut on the far side of the airfield and we kicked our heels around.'

George did manage to get in a few ferry trips (Ansons, Mosquitoes, Dakotas), but the idea of a Met Flight fell through and 'after a long period of hanging about I found myself at the Almaza transit camp just outside Cairo, before being posted to No. 132 Maintenance Unit at RAF Ismailia in the canal zone. He remembers:

On reporting to the Flight Office I enquired as to what went on there and was informed that in the main they were testing Spitfires ready for sale to the Greek Air Force. I informed the chief pilot that I was a multi-engine pilot and had not flown a single-engine aircraft since my Tiger Moth days. His reply was to sling across the desk a copy of Spitfire Pilot Notes with the comment, 'you'll soon pick it up!' Various aircraft came through the MU and for the first three weeks I was flying Mosquitos, Proctors, Fairchild Arguses and Ansons. Then on 25 April came the big day when I had the great pleasure of taking to the air in a Spitfire. Little did I imagine when in 1940 I witnessed the dog fights over Kent that one day I would have the opportunity of flying one. It was great feeling being

able to throw it around the sky at will. Subsequently I flew
a Hurricane and a Mustang.

(In January 1947 George tested a Spitfire Mk IX, MJ755, which
subsequently was flown to Greece to join the Greek Air Force.
Seventy-two years later he would meet this aircraft again.)

Finally, I was called over to a tented camp at Kilo 40 to check
out a number of Halifax bombers with the Hercules engines,
as surprisingly they could not trace any other Halifax pilot
in the area at that time. During my time in the Middle East
I managed three ferry trips to the UK – once with a Mosquito
and twice with a Halifax, the last being my final trip at the
controls of an aircraft before being demobbed.

Chapter Seven

Typical Air Force

'For the first week after being screened', Ferris wrote, 'I was acting Engineer Leader as he was on leave. ... This was a job I didn't like. The first night an engineer went sick and I had to find a spare or go myself. I found one who had not got a crew yet. He did look quite nervous, so I went with him to briefing and out to the kite. Gave him all the gen I knew. Felt quite sorry for him. Felt worse the next morning as he was with a crew who were reported missing.' During this time Ferris's mother threw a party for the crew. 'Had a very nice evening. After dinner did a spot of dancing and Reg did a spot of singing with the band. Finished up at Moorhouses with Stella and Cath rather pixilated and my mother not looking at all pleased. Anyway you don't celebrate the end of a tour of ops every week.'

On 16 October Ferris found himself posted to No. 1638 Heavy Conversion Unit at RAF Riccall. 'A wartime drome but not too bad.' Ferris took up a role as a flying instructor. 'So it's back to where I started except I'm doing the instructing now. ... Didn't do a lot of flying, managed to get home fairly often. ... Used to fly over to Carnaby for two and three engine landings and over shoots.' He continued:

Had one little experience on Jan 4th landing at Marston

Moor. Quite a strong cross wind blowing and on landing the kite shot off the runway to starboard. We finished up on the grass but apart from giving us a good shaking we were OK.

Reg rang up one afternoon from Marston Moor to tell me that George and himself had been awarded gongs. Came home for a day off shortly afterwards, the 16 February 1944, and on arrival home found my photo and a bottle of Champagne waiting for me on the table. I wondered what had happened. It had been in the *Yorkshire Post* that morning [the award of Ferris's Distinguished Flying Medal], so they knew about it before me. Spent rest of the morning answering phone from friends ringing in to congratulate me.

4 March, a ground instructor's job was wanting filling at St. Athan Flight Engineers School. So the Engineer Leader picked on me to go. Why me I wouldn't know. I know nobody wanted to go down there and I expect he picked the one who would make the least fuss about going. I went OK. Never said a word (couldn't anyway) not even goodbye. I always thought he did the dirty on me. They always say if you don't want a bloke get him posted.

On 6 March Ferris arrived at No. 4 School of Technical Training, St Athan, and 'had an interview with the Wingco in charge'.

I told him I didn't care for the job, didn't think I had had the necessary experience for giving instruction, and in view of the short time I was working as a fitter before I did my flight engineer course he quite agreed with me. So he put me in Maintenance Flight doing clerical work until he could get me a posting. I was there three weeks during which I had a pleasant time.

I gave a talk to the flight engineers under training on 'what happens to me when I reach an HCU'. I went round the section and talked to some of the old instructors who were

still there. They used to say they liked to see some of the
old faces back as it gave the budding engineers a lot more
confidence. Sort of feeling that if that silly devil can get
through a tour of ops I'm sure I can.

On the last week of my stay I had a letter from home telling
me that Ronnie Thornton was posted missing. He always used
to say, 'How about coming into my crew if I can get you
transferred. You'll be much safer on Lancs you know.' I'm
afraid flak and fighters can shoot down any kind of plane if
they can hit me.

April 1944 found Ferris Newton at RAF Hawarden, and No. 48
Maintenance Unit Test Flight, under the command of a Flight
Lieutenant Duffy. 'Nice easy hours -- no night flying or anything
like that. Only duty we had was to Orderly Sergeant, which didn't
come round very often. I only had it to do once whilst I was there.'
He continued:

Another job we had to do (I say we – the three Flight
Engineers) was to take the Wing Commander's personal
friends and relations round the aircraft. Also quite a lot of
Americans, and as there was an Air Transport Auxiliary ferry
pool over the other side of the drome, where there was always
at least a dozen different types of aircraft in, it used to get a
little embarrassing, some of the aircraft I'd never seen before.
I used to steer my little parties to old faithfuls Halifax, Lancs,
Stirling, Wellington.

The Yanks, of course, used to leave boxes of Cammel's
cartons of sweets and piles of gum after a visit, and I can see
old Duffy now sharing it all into eight equal piles. Why eight
when only we three engineers did it I don't know – well of
course I do really. He had two rings up. We had some good
fun though all the same, Went on a good few cycle rides with
Helen and Fifield.

In mid-July Ferris was posted to No. 6 Maintenance Unit at RAF Brize Norton, to convert on to Stirlings:

Only one other flight engineer and four pilots in Test Flight. Brize Norton was a huge place with a lot of gliders and Parachute Men.

Had my first flight in a Stirling on the 17th for one hour, had another hour the next day. After that the flight engineer and Stirling pilots posted. Typical Air Force, send me here to get Stirling experience then post all the pilots and engineers. Nothing for me to do now as none of the other pilots could fly a Stirling, so I asked for a 48 hour pass, which started on Friday 1615 and finished at 1030 Tuesday. Best '48' hour pass I ever had. When I got back found I had to go to Woburn.

On 27 July 1944 Ferris arrived at No. 34 Satellite Landing Ground, Woburn Park:

That's all there was. It was situated in Woburn Park on the Duke of Bedford's Estate, complete with deer and what have you.

All the Stirlings were parked all over the park under trees etc. These Stirlings were all for the use of Airborne troops or glider towing. The flight office was a mobile caravan. Flight Lieutenant Hindley was the CO. … All the ground crews came from a nearby aerodrome by bus every day. The flying types were in civvy billets in Woburn village. I lived with a Mr and Mrs Smith. Very nice it was too. Cup of tea in bed in the morning, then a short walk down to the park. Nice easy hours, no night flying, that seems to be a thing of the past. The last time I did any was on the 28th November 1943.

We had about 80 Stirlings to look after, we just used to take them up for about half an hour, test everything and then park them up again. We used to average about five flights a day.

Ferris recalls that Woburn Abbey itself had been turned into a 'bird cage' for Wrens (women serving with the Women's Royal Naval Service). 'The dear little things used to go out onto the flat roof to sun bathe. Of course it didn't takes the 'wolves' in the park long to start low flying over the Abbey rooftops. The Chief Wren soon put a complaint in to Flight Lieutenant Hindley; best of it was he was one of the culprits. Needless to say it had to stop as of course it really could have been dangerous.'

Following ten days of leave Ferris was back at Woburn Park, and for 17 September, the day of the launch of Operation Market Garden – the towing of gliders and the dropping of airborne troops to capture key bridges in Holland – Ferris recalled:

All was peace and joy (as we lay back in comfort and thought of those poor chaps being dropped) until Tuesday the 19th.

The CO received a signal to prepare as many aircraft as possible for immediate take over by ATA. In flew the old Anson and out popped about four or five ferry pilots including one woman. They took about twenty away the first day. They came again the next day, more of them this time, and another thirty went. So it was looking like goodbye to Woburn before very long now. September the 20th was my last time I went up, tested three that day and that was that. By the 24th I was on my way to Transport Command HQ.

At interview Ferris was told that following three months at a heavy conversion unit instructing, he would be crewed up and able to go out on the routes. 'It all sounded very nice but it certainly took more than three months to get out onto the routes.' At No. 1332 HCU RAF Longtown Ferris was 'kept hanging around for a few days until they decided to send the pilots and engineers down to Winthorpe to do a Stirling academy course. As if we all hadn't done enough courses. Oh well keep us all out of mischief. That being the main reason for this new course.' At Winthorpe Ferris 'only once went

to the engineer's section, the rest of the time I kept out of the way
unless I was flying. Well there was no point in going and looking
for work. Went to Newark a few times, bought Cath a Ronson lighter
whilst I was there.' On 9 October Ferris was posted back to
Longtown. 'Before I left Winthorpe spoke to Cath and told her we
should be changing stations at Leeds so arranged for her to be there.
Had a few words with her, because she asked me who the untidy
looking chap with me was. When I told her he was my skipper she
nearly had a fit. Arrived back at Longtown to find all the rest of the
unit had gone over to Ireland. On the 11th October Squadron Leader
Sach came over in a Liberator and took the rest of us over to the
island over the sea.' On 11 October 1944 Ferris arrived at RAF Nutts
Corner. 'Landed on Irish soil for the first time at 1206. What a place
this was, wartime drome of course, dispersals all over the place.
Luckily I managed to get a bike fairly quickly.' A short bus ride
offered the chance to visit Belfast but 'trouble was getting the time
off ... we certainly had to put some hours in.'

> The unit was divided into three flights. I went into 'A' Flight. A
> crew would come in off one of the other Commands, the pilot
> was put through a course in 'A' Flight, and whilst he was con-
> verting onto Stirlings the rest of his crew, engineer and wop
> and navigator, did a ground course in their respective sections.
> That's where we came in, screened engineer and wop, we had
> to fly with the pupil pilot. Not too bad when the pupil had an
> instructor pilot with him, but when he used to send him off
> solo yours truly and the wop had to stay with him. We had
> some real shaky dos. I think I had more narrow shaves during
> the next three months than I did when I was on ops. Examples.
>   Night flying, first solo landing. Touch down, swing, off the
> runway we charged, down to the axles in mud. Poor Bill the
> wop who was sat at this wireless set and didn't know what was
> happening got the shock of his life.
>   Night flying. Flight Lieutenant Ross first solo landing on

the short runway as well. Touch down nearly halfway down
the runway. We bounced up in the air. Couldn't possibly land
it so I said better do an overshoot and did the necessary
operations. I don't know whether he was going to do that or
not but I wasn't taking any chances, so I did it for him. Swing
on take-off – off the runway she goes, the pilot tries to keep
her going by giving more throttle but that only drives her
deeper into the mud where she struck with the tail in the air
and her nose in the ground. Nobody hurt. Bags of fun and
games. They said that if you could fly a Stirling you could fly
any other kite there was. More pilots from pilot officers to
squadron leaders were getting scrubbed off the course than
I was having Irish eggs (and I was getting plenty). Squadron
Leader Wicht, DSO, DFC, he was off; written a Stirling off
as well. Made a bad landing and tore the undercarriage off.

On exercise 9 cross-country. … Flying over the north of
Scotland. Port outer engineer started coaring, that is the
freezing up of oil radiator, giving high oil temperature and
very low pressure. I reported to the pilot and he came back
with, 'What's that engineer?' I ignored that and told him what
to do, 'reduce revs to 1800 on port outer', which he did. After a
short time it gave no indication of returning to normal. 'You
must reduce your air speed more, suggest you lower under
cart and put on one third flap.' 'Port outer no improvement
and port inner now coaring, suggest you feather port outer
and reduce revs on all engines.'

'Any improvement engineer?'

'Not yet skipper. I think the best plan is to ask the nav to
give you a course to the nearest drome.'

This was done and it was found that the nearest was our
own so we turned for home.

'Slight improvement on port inner skipper', and then later,
'take flap in and undercarriage up skipper, temperature and
pressure returning to normal.'

I think that was one of the worst cross-countries I'd ever been on, two engines on one side coaring a bit much and a pilot who had never heard of coaring.

Two days later I went on the same cross-country, this time I was with Flight Lieutenant Grant, we had coaring three times on the port inner. He hadn't a clue on the procedure to adopt either. After that they decided to put a plate on the oil radiators and all the pilots had a lecture on coaring. It was only a night or two before that, that a kite disappeared in the sea perhaps from the same thing. It was a lousy cross-country that one, straight out over the Atlantic for about three hours, then turn and find Rockall, a small bit of rock sticking out of the sea NNW of Scotland, and then back to base. A real test for the navigator.

Five days later, on 9 November, Ferris had news to report for an investiture at Buckingham Palace, and to tell Cath and his mother they would need to get there early to get a decent seat to watch proceedings. 'I felt very thrilled and excited, I could hardly wait to get home.'

On Monday the three of us went down to London. We stayed at the Regent Palace. Had not been in bed very long before we had an air raid warning. I was for staying where we were, but Cath thought perhaps mother would feel safer in the hotel shelter, so off we all went. There were quite a good few people in the shelter and we had to stay there about half an hour. It had been a flying bomb raid.

The next morning we were up early, and I gave my buttons an extra shine. Took a taxi to the Palace, arriving there about 1015. I left Cath and Mother to go into the Grand Hall whilst I went into another room, after depositing my hat and coat in a cloakroom. One of the Palace officials checked my name off on a long list and put a fishhook in my tunic. That is so the King can just hook the medal onto it without having to pin it himself. By about 1030 the room was pretty full of service types and civilians. The ladies were taken off into another smaller room so that they may practice [sic] curtsying. One of the Court officials gave the men the gen on what to do. We were then all put into order to correspond with their lists, Victoria Cross first and so on down the scale of awards.

At eleven o'clock the queue started to move slowly out of the room along a passage and into the Grand Hall, where half way down one side there was a raised dais with the King standing there in Naval uniform surrounded by other officers of the services. I scan the crowd of seated relatives and friends and I saw Cath and Mother three rows from the front, bang in front of the dais. Beefeaters stand along the walls at about five yard intervals, and the string section of one of the Guards bands plays in the background.

My turn is coming up quick now, standing at the bottom of the runway is a Naval officer who again checks your name. From there you go to the top of the dais, stand there whilst the Lord Chamberlain calls out.

'Sergeant Newton. DFM. Bomber Command.'

Go forward, stop, turn left, bow, step one pace forward and you're face to face with the King. He takes the medal off a purple cushion, without looking for it, handed to him by one of his officers, puts it on the fish hook and shakes your hand. Whilst this had been going on the King said, 'How many operations have you done?'

'Twenty-nine sir.'

'The best of luck.'

Step back one pace, bow, turn right, and walk off the runway at the far end. At the bottom another official is waiting to give you your box with your name on to put your medal in.

After that I went to the back of the hall and watched the rest of the people decorated, as of course nobody can leave until it is all over. When it was finished, I went out and found

Dennis waiting to see me. Had our photo taken for the *Yorks Post*, and then we all went up to the Trocadero for lunch. Mother and Cath caught the afternoon train for home and I went for the train for Stranraer and Nutts Corner.

A few days later Ferris was told by his flight commander that he was going to be recommended for a commission. 'He didn't know why I hadn't had one before.' On 24 November Ferris had his interview with the wing commander. 'It seemed a fairly satisfactory interview, but you can never tell.' After some leave it was time for an interview with the station commander. 'I didn't think that interview went at all well. I felt very uncomfortable. He didn't like my home address for one thing. He kept coming back to it. What kind of place was it? Did I own it? Was it residential etc etc? And of course my schooling or lack of it left much to be desired if I was to become an officer and a gentleman. So I was not really surprised that I had to see the adjutant on the 13th February. He told me the "glad tidings" – my commission temporarily suspended by Group Captain, try again in three months' time. That of course didn't mean a thing, I have had it I'm afraid.' However, for 23 March Ferris was able to record, 'Change of rank, now Warrant Officer', and a couple of weeks later, 'Put into "B" Flight. Now flying on Yorks. Nice change from Stirlings. No more cross-country flights.' Ferris added, perhaps with a subtext of relief, 'I now get out when the pilot instructor does, leaving the pupils to carry on on their own.'

A month later and the war was over. On 8 May, VE Day, Ferris ventured into Belfast: 'The place was packed, everyone just walking the street. Glad to get back to camp.' A couple of days later and, along with his unit, Ferris was posted back to Riccall. Similar duties followed, including a spell as orderly officer. 'I couldn't help but smile thinking of the time not very long ago when I was an Erk myself. At 1800 hours I had to inspect the defaulters' parade at the Guard Room. That didn't take very long.' During July, and following a posting to RAF Leconfield, Ferris prepared to head east. 'Had our yellow fever jabs, which didn't have any bad effects on me, thank goodness. ... Issued with tropical kit, shall get my knees brown after all. A scheme introduced to take any ground staff across to the other side so they could see the bomb damage. We took a party over on the 26 July and went over Emden, Bremen, Hamburg, Kiel, Heligoland. First time I'd seen it in daylight.'

At the end of the month Ferris flew to Castel Benito in North Africa. On arrival, and after reporting to flying control, 'we went down for a cup of tea. The heat and the flies. I don't know which was the worst, the flies or the heat.' On return to the UK, and some local cross-country flying, Ferris's next overseas duty involved a flight to Karachi. Starting on 22 September, 'The only snag to us was the fact that the Wing Commander had decided to go with us.' They initially picked up fourteen soldiers and kit from St Mawgan, and that evening Ferris's crew, 'all went down to Newquay with the Wingco, who didn't seem half as bad as what we had expected.' They took off from Castel Benito, then on to Lydda in Palestine, Shiabah, and finally Karachi. 'Total flying time for the trip of 23 hours and 20 minutes, taking four days to do it.' Facilities at Karachi, however, did not impress. Ferris was billeted, 'on number 9 site, under canvas too'.

What a dump it was, the mess was filthy and the food terrible. We thought good job we are not stopping here long. Our hopes were doomed next morning, went up to the main camp and found that one of our petrol tanks had got a leak. That meant we should be stuck there until they could send another out from the UK. We went back to the transit camp feeling very depressed. We were looking forward to having a chance to have a look around Karachi but not staying on number 9 site. We said we would try it one more day and if there was no improvement we would tell Bluie [Ferris's pilot] about it. It was no better, so we told Bluie and he told the Wingco who came over to have a look for himself. Went back and told them his crew couldn't stay there, they had better find them a better site than that. We finished up being put on the permanent staff site. It's useful to have a Wing Commander in one's crew now and again. I have never in my Air Force life seen such a dump as that was.

After nine days, 'of hanging around and one or two trips down to Karachi we eventually got away – empty'. Arriving at Shiabah they picked up some airmen going on leave, taking them to Lydda, where they collected some ex-POWs from the Japanese conflict. 'Those who were well enough to stand the air journey came by Transport Command. They had a stop of 48 hours in Lydda for climation [sic].' Via Castel Benito Ferris arrived back in the UK. 'Went on leave with bananas, nuts, shoes, nylons, chocolate, etc, etc.' On return he flew again to Karachi, on 27 October, this time via Cairo West, arriving there early in the morning and scheduled for an overnight stay. 'Had a quick wash and brush up and out to the main road to thumb a lift into Cairo. We were hounded to death by the street urchins, pick pockets, and guides to everywhere from dancing girls in the nude to picture post cards. We were so fed up that after lunch we went to see a football match in the Army barracks. The trouble was we all looked too white – sort of straight out from England that we were easy prey for the Arab spivs.'

Once in Karachi, they prepared for their return, 'with a load of ex-POWs from Japan. On the Shiabah–Lydda leg we had to turn back after an hour and a half owing to a bad storm. The poor passengers looked very fed up when they got out of the kite and found they were back where they started. Left the next night – no trouble this time.'

In January 1946 Ferris found himself at No. 51 Squadron, RAF Stradishall, involved in converting the squadron on to Yorks. 'Our first pupil was of course our new CO, Wing Commander Iveson. … After the Wingco was going solo we started on the flight commanders.' Ferris recalled one notable incident on 21 March:

York aircraft in circuits and bumps. … Port inner engine temp. going off the clock and lot of smoke coming out of the engine.

'Looks as though the P.I. is on fire engineer, better feather and press fire button.'

'OK skipper.'

I feathered and pressed the fire button, which sprays the whole of the engine with foam. Pilot calls up the control tower.

'L Love calling port inner engine on fire, making emergency landing.'

We do a half turn cutting normal circuit and land with the fire tender and blood wagon following us down the runway. Still quite a bit of smoke coming out. We roll to a stop at the end of the runway, everything looks under control, hardly any smoke coming out now. The blood wagon turns off disappointed, the skipper decides to taxi her round to dispersal, the fire tender following round. The fire was caused by a fault in a petrol pipe. First time I had been in a kite and had an engine on fire.

On 4 April 1946 Ferris had his release medical, writing in his memoir, 'So it won't be long now dear reader, that's if you're still with me.' And on 24 April, 'Did my last flight in the Service at 1400 hours. That was just to bring my total flying hours to top the thousand.' On 4 May, 'Told I should be going to the release centre on 6 May, so started to hand my kit in. Made my final clearance chit out.' And so it was two days later, 'Reported to Uxbridge.'

First went into a large room where they were serving cups of tea and cakes. Sat there until they call your name through the Tannoy. A walk across the road into an even larger hall. The first thing one gets is an FFI. After that you start the round visiting all the various tables, issued with my cards (at last) through Accounts drawing about £30 the rest to be sent on. The final touch being said goodbye to by an officer, not forgetting to tell you that the Air Force would be pleased to have you back. YOU WHAT?

Getting cleared through took about an hour. From there we were taken by bus to Wembley to be issued with our demob suits. From there it's home James and don't spare the horses.

Chapter Eight

Post-war and Reflections

George Dunn flew forty-four operational sorties during the war, Ferris flew twenty-nine. George had been keen to do his bit, as had Ferris. Both had remained resolute and both had been decorated. When Ferris left the Royal Air Force he took over the running of the family business. Eventually he would retire to the east coast of Yorkshire, not too far from Holme-on-Spalding-Moor, with his second wife. Sadly, after suffering a major stroke, Ferris died at the age of seventy-four.

When George left the RAF he took a course at the London School of Air Navigation and obtained his commercial licence, 'but there were so many pilots on the market that it was almost impossible to get a job in flying. In my digs alone there were nineteen of us! I decided to give up on the idea and returned to Pickfords, the Removal Company who I was with when the war broke out. I started again as a branch manager at Herne Bay and subsequently at Nelson, Lancs, then Aldershot and finally at Hove until I retired at Christmas 1982. During this period, I became National Chairman of the Institute of the Furniture and Warehousing Industry for one year in 1978.'

Recently George had the opportunity to become acquainted with one of his previous steeds:

> I was invited to a Veterans Day at Biggin Hill and on entering
> the Heritage hangar I noticed a young engineer working on
> the early stages of assembling a Spitfire fuselage, of an aircraft
> which had arrived in pieces from Athens. A small plaque on
> a stand gave its brief history and it rang a bell with me as in
> January 1947 I was stationed at No. 107 Maintenance Unit,
> Kasfareet, Egypt, testing Spitfires for sale to the Greek Air
> Force. On checking my logbook I found that I had tested this
> aircraft, Spitfire Mark IX MJ 755, on 28 January 1947 shortly
> before its transfer to Greece the following month. The
> authorities at Biggin Hill passed this information to the
> Curator of the Greek Museum and he kindly sent me a nice
> framed photo of the aircraft when it was on display outside
> the Museum. It is owned by the Icarus Foundation and is
> still at Biggin Hill having been completely restored, and
> I have had the pleasure of seeing it flying again.

Ferris wrote down his thoughts about serving with Bomber
Command, and in particular Sir Arthur Harris.

> Bert Harris, to give him the nickname that his brother officers
> called him, has been built up to the ruthlessly efficient
> commander of a force of destruction intent upon his objective
> irrespective of the cost. One correspondent commenting on
> his approaching retirement said that he was known as 'Butch'
> in the RAF, short for butcher. That is not the picture of the
> Harris that I know.
> In this war Harris fought for his command and the boys
> who flew the bombers. He had to fight those opposed to the
> bombing strategy, and there were many. Under his command
> the thousand bomber raid became a possibility, instead of a
> dream, and Churchill, convinced of the powers of the bomber,

backed it, and the four-engine bomber got manpower priority. Through his persistence new devices were developed to improve bombing accuracy and new tactics were developed to reduce losses.

In his heart Harris mourned the loss of the gallant fellows whose lives were lost flying his bombers. But he knew he had to keep his thoughts to himself and guard his speech, for on his manner depended the morale of the whole command. Some shy little pig-tailed Jacqueline Harris will grow up and realise that her daddy was a great war leader. Perhaps the British public will grow up too, and understand that Harris's policy saved countless lives in the Army and Navy and among British civilians, and that no man contributed more to the reduction of Allied casualties in the Second Great War.

George looks back with fond memories of his time with Bomber Command:

I enjoyed my service career, but it was a great pity that it took a war to give me the opportunity of a terrific flying experience that I would otherwise never have had.

I feel it was something that had to be done. It wasn't a question of revenge but Harris had the right idea. Let's bomb their factories, their installations, anything that is contributing towards their war effort, and I always felt that it had to be done. Unfortunately in all wars you are going to get innocent victims. It didn't worry me unduly, it's unfortunate but when you think back to all the casualties we had in Coventry and London, thousands of civilians [were] killed.

In 2012 The Bomber Command Memorial was unveiled by Her Majesty Queen Elizabeth II in The Green Park, London. To raise funds for the memorial, and its upkeep, the Bomber Command Aircrew Veterans Group (Sussex), of which George was a part, came into being in 2009. To date over £100,000 has been raised and the group's achievement was recognised with a 'Special Recognition' award from the Royal Air Force Benevolent Fund. Sadly, so many of George's colleagues, whose sterling work ensured the memorial was built, have passed away. George is one of the last remaining members of the group, and he continues to support the fundraising of the RAFBF, who maintain the memorial. In an interview carried out a few months prior to the official unveiling of the memorial, George stated: 'I think it is a wonderful idea. When you think of the contribution that Bomber Command made to the war effort, it must have shortened the war considerably. Bomber Command got a bad press. But I think now, these chaps would be looking down and saying, "At last we've got some recognition".'

Appendix 1
George Dunn's Operational Logbook Entries

Sortie	Date	Sqdn	Base	Aircraft	Target	Flight Time
1	3 April 1943 [Second-dickey trip.]	10	RAF Melbourne	Halifax 'H' DT791	Essen	4.45 hours
2	4 April 1943 [Second-dickey trip.]	10	RAF Melbourne	Halifax 'E' HR695	Kiel	5.35 hours
3	23 May 1943 Uneventful – clear.	76	RAF Linton-on-Ouse	Halifax 'J'	Dortmund	7.05 hours
4	25 May 1943 Good trip. Scattered cloud. No S/Ls.	76	RAF Linton-on-Ouse	Halifax 'J	Düsseldorf	5.15 hours
5	27 May 1943 Good trip. 8/10 cloud – very heavy flak. Good concentration of fires.	76	RAF Linton-on-Ouse	Halifax 'J'	Essen	5.45 hours.
6	29 May 1943 Uneventful – fires concentrated.	76	RAF Linton-on-Ouse	Halifax 'J'	Wuppertal	5.40 hours.
7	11 June 1943 Uneventful. Good effort and results OK. No camera carried.	76	RAF Linton-on-Ouse	Halifax 'J',	Düsseldorf	6.15 hours
8	12 June 1943 7/10ths cloud over target. Results good.	76	RAF Linton-on-Ouse	Halifax 'J'	Bochum	5.45 hours.
9	21 June 1943 Good trip. Fires very concentrated. Defences fairly weak.	76	RAF Holme-on-Spalding-Moor	Halifax 'G'	Krefeld	4.25 hrs.
10	22 June 1943 3/10 cloud over target – results seen were good – usual Ruhr activity.	76	RAF Holme-on-Spalding-Moor	Halifax 'G'	Mulheim	4.30 hours
11	24 June 1943 10/10 cloud in T/A although target clear. Flak very heavy and numerous S/Ls. Results good.	76	RAF Holme-on-Spalding-Moor	Halifax 'G'	Wuppertal	4.55 hours
12	25 June 1943 10/10 Cloud. Intense flak but S/Ls ineffective. Detailed for Special Recco Report.	76	RAF Holme-on-Spalding-Moor	Halifax 'G'	Gelsenkirchen	4.40 hours

Sortie	Date	Sqdn	Base	Aircraft	Target	Flight Time
13	28 June 1943	76	RAF Holme-on-Spalding-Moor	Halifax 'G'	Cologne	4.50 hours

10/10 cloud. Heavy barrage flak. Caught in flak on way back. S/Ls ineffective. Fires seen.

| 14 | 3 July 1943 | 76 | RAF Holme-on-Spalding-Moor | Halifax 'G' | Cologne | 5.20 hours |

3/10 cloud. Intense flak. Good results.

| 15 | 9 July 1943 | 76 | RAF Holme-on-Spalding-Moor | Halifax 'G' | Gelsenkirchen | 6.05 hours |

10/10 cloud. Heavy barrage flak. No results observed.

| 16 | 13 July 1943 | 76 | RAF Holme-on-Spalding-Moor | Halifax 'G' | Aachen | 5.05 hours |

8/10 cloud. Flak weak – no S/Ls. Accurate results not observed.

| 17 | 15 July 1943 | 76 | RAF Holme-on-Spalding-Moor | Halifax 'G' | Montbéliard | 7.55 hours |

Few defences. Good photo & astro fixes.

| 18 | 29 July 1943 | 76 | RAF Holme-on-Spalding-Moor | Halifax 'A' | Hamburg | 5.40 hours |

Numerous S/Ls. Flak moderate. Good prang.

| 19 | 30 July 1943 | 76 | RAF Holme-on-Spalding-Moor | Halifax 'A' | Remscheid | 5.40 hours |

Clear weather – target defences weak – very good results. Saw 4 shot down.

| 20 | 2 August 1943 | 76 | RAF Holme-on-Spalding-Moor | Halifax 'A' | Hamburg | 5.25 hours |

Encountered severe electrical storm. Heavy icing & severe static conditions. Jettisoned bombs 14 mins before ETA.

| 21 | 9 August 1943 | 76 | RAF Holme-on-Spalding-Moor | Halifax 'B' | Mannheim | 6.40 hours |

Good trip. Defences ineffective.

| 22 | 12 August 1943 | 76 | RAF Holme-on-Spalding-Moor | Halifax 'B' | Milan, | 9.25 hours |

Uneventful trip. Defences weak. Over the Alps in moonlight!!

| 23 | 17 August 1943 | 76 | RAF Holme-on-Spalding-Moor | Halifax 'G' | Peenemünde | 7.40 hours |

Brilliant moonlight – good trip. Diverted to Wymeswold. Secret research station.

| 24 | 22 August 1943 | 76 | RAF Holme-on-Spalding-Moor | Halifax 'G' | Leverkusen | 5.00 hours |

10/10 cloud. Intense flak. No S/Ls. PFF u/s.

| 25 | 23 August 1943 | 76 | RAF Holme-on-Spalding-Moor | Halifax 'G' | Berlin | 8.05 hours |

Largest so far. Clear target. Moderate flak – many S/Ls. Very successful raid. Diverted to Catfoss owing to weather.

Sortie	Date	Sqdn	Base	Aircraft	Target	Flight Time
26	6 Sept 1943	76	RAF Holme-on-Spalding-Moor	Halifax 'G'	Munich	8.35 hours
	Defences moderate. Results good. Landed at Hartford Bridge. Fuel shortage.					
27	15 Sept 1943	76	RAF Holme-on-Spalding-Moor	Halifax 'G'	Montluçon,	6.40 hours
	Rubber tyre factory. Good prang. No defences. 8/10 cloud.					
28	16 Sept 1943	76	RAF Holme-on-Spalding-Moor	Halifax 'G'	Modane	7.05 hours
	Returned when 30 mins of target ETA. Severe icing & ASI failure.					
29	29 Sept 1943	76	RAF Holme-on-Spalding-Moor	Halifax 'G'	Bochum	4.55 hours
	T/A clear. Flak moderate – numerous S/Ls. Very successful raid. Special Recco Report.					
30	3 October 1943	76,	RAF Holme-on-Spalding-Moor	Halifax 'G'	Kassel	6.35 hours
	Good results. Defences moderate. Special Recco Report. 4 a/c from Sqdn lost.					
31	1 March 1945	608	RAF Downham Market	Mosquito 'H' KB347	Berlin	5.10 hours
	4 x 500lb, flak hits on spinners.					
32	3 March 1945	608	RAF Downham Market	Mosquito 'G' KB355	Berlin	4.25 hours
	4 x 500lb.					
33	5 March 1945	608	RAF Downham Market	Mosquito 'G' KB355	Berlin	4.50 hours
	4 x 500lb diverted to L Staughton.					
34	7 March 1945	608	RAF Downham Market	Mosquito 'B' KB146	Berlin	4.35 hours
	3 x 500lb, 1 x 500lb LD.					
35	8 March 1945	608	RAF Downham Market	Mosquito 'G' KB355	Berlin	4.30 hours
	3 x 500lb, 1 x 500lb LD.					
36	10 March 1945	608	RAF Downham Market	Mosquito 'B' KB356	Berlin	4.20 hours
	3 x 500lb, 1 x 500lb LD.					
37	12 March 1945	608	RAF Downham Market	Mosquito 'G' KB355	Berlin	4.20 hours
	2 x 500lb, 2 x 500lb LD.					
38	13 March 1945	608	RAF Downham Market	Mosquito 'B' KB356	Berlin	4.10 hours
	3 x 500lb, 1 x 500lb LD.					

Sortie	Date	Sqdn	Base	Aircraft	Target	Flight Time
39	15 March 1945	608	RAF Downham Market	Mosquito 'G' KB355	Erfurt	4.45 hours
	3 x 500lb, 3 Flares.					
40	17 March 1945	608	RAF Downham Market	Mosquito 'D' KB417	Berlin	4.05 hours
	3 x 500lb, 1 x 500lb LD.					
41	29 March 1945	608,	RAF Downham Market	Mosquito 'C' KB493	Berlin	4.20 hours
	2 x 500lb, 2 x 500lb LD.					

Sortie	Date	Unit	Base	Aircraft	Target	Flight Time
42	9 April 1945	1409 Met Flight	RAF Wyton	Mosquito 'A' 786	Kiel	4.30 hours
	Pre-Met recce & snooper on Kiel. VHF Met to M.B. Cine camera used.					
43	14 April 1945	1409 Met Flight	RAF Wyton	Mosquito 'F' 734	Pampa	4.35 hours
	Base–Wells–Stodd–Stettin–Celle–Den Helder–Base					
44	16 April 1945	1409 Met Flight	RAF Wyton	Mosquito 'C' 733	Pampa	3.20 hours
	Base–Wells–DR–Bremen–DR–Cuxhaven–DR–Wells.					

Appendix 11
Air Ministry Bulletin, No. 1409 Flight, 1945

Air Ministry News Service   Air Ministry Bulletin – No. 17031

BOMBER COMMAND'S METEOROLOGICAL FLIGHT

MEN PICKED TO FLY THROUGH WEATHER

Every hour of the twenty-four, two Mosquitos and their crews are waiting at a
R.A.F. Bomber Command Station, ready to take off to anywhere from the Arctic
Circle to the Mediterranean, even in weather when no other aircraft will be flying.

These aircraft belong to the Meteorological Flight, manned by a small body of
some of the most experienced airmen of the R.A.F.

For three years they have flown over Germany, before every major attack by
Bomber Command and, until recently, before every U.S.A.A.F.

They are men who challenge the weather at its worst.

If they see an icing cloud which any other pilot would avoid, they go out of
their way to fly through it. They are prepared to break cloud at a height of a few feet
above Germany, and to fly the rest of their way home at tree-top level, or to make
blind landing in fog, or with the cloud almost down to the surface of the airfield.

Moreover it is their tradition that they never refuse a flight. And it was recently
found that the average number of operational flights by each member of the
Flight was eighty-seven, and that the Flight had won as many awards as there were
men in it.

They probably do more actual flying over enemy territory than any other
formation of the R.A.F.

In fact, 24 or 25 trips a month for each crew is usual.

When H.M. The King flew to Italy, a Mosquito of this Flight went ahead to keep
a watch on the weather. Mosquitos of this Flight have also been detailed to go ahead
of Mr. Churchill.

In September 1941, a question about the weather over the Continent arose, and it
could not be answered by any of the ordinary weather reconnaissance over enemy
territory. That was the beginning of this Met. Flight Unit, which for some time
operated with R.A.F. Coastal Command – since more and more of its flights were
made to obtain information for forecasting the weather for bomber operations,
in the Spring of 1943 it was transferred to Bomber Command, and placed under
Pathfinder Force.

The Flight used to fly Mosquito IXs, but later was equipped with pressure cabin
Mosquito XVIs, which it now flies.

A Met. flight over Germany is normally planned so that the Mosquito lands
some time before the heavy bombers are due to take off. But this is not always
possible, and there have been instances where an operation was cancelled five minutes before take-off time or even after the bombers were airborne, on a report of a
Met. Flight pilot.

Security is the constant preoccupation of everyone associated with the Met.

Flight because it is so much concerned with future operations.

Its busiest week, for example, was just before D-Day, when its aircraft were constantly over the Atlantic. Reports of the men of this flight helped decide the fate of the *Tirpitz*.

They fly over Germany by night as well as day. In the darkness, they often use flares to light up the clouds and observe their height, one of the main questions which crews have to answer.

The aircraft carry several cameras, and their crews photograph not only the weather, but also anything in enemy territory that may be of value to the Intelligence Section of the R.A.F. A photograph taken by an aircraft of this flight, for example, led to an attack by the U.S.A.A.F. a short time after on the V Weapon Research Station at Peenemünde. Photographs are always developed within half an hour of landing.

Routes must be well planned, yet in the shortest possible time, so that the Met. Flight navigators have a great responsibility, and crews are carefully briefed on the type of meteorological information required.

The crews seldom fly to an actual target for a pending operation, but to a point from which the weather, as it will be over the target, is coming. A comprehensive picture of the weather over the whole route, rather than a series of disconnected observations, is what is needed. Pilot and navigator prepare their report together as they fly home, and are ready on landing, to give a brief, accurate, and clear report before the main force takes off. If the report is urgently required it may be sent back in code by wireless. Otherwise, the crew reports by special telephone on a hook-up to Command and Group Met. Officers. For this, all crews are trained to make concise reports on a telephone hook-up before they begin their work.

Though all the men in the Met. Flight have had at least one operational tour, or equivalent experience in reconnaissance work, during which they learn meteorological theory and photography, as well as making many practice flights.

The atmosphere in the Met. Flight is somewhat different from that of an ordinary Bomber Station. Apart from actual leave, there is very little time when the crew can actually leave the station. They must be available for a call at any moment of the 24 hours. Therefore they have to be men who can get on with each other, and the Flight Commander chooses them as if he were selecting men for an expedition to the arctic, where friction must be avoided. The ground-crews must also be available at all times to service the aircraft, for there are no intervals between Met. flights comparable to those between normal operations. They never know where the Mosquitos fly, either before or after the sorties; and in spite of this their team spirit is remarkable.

Sources and Acknowledgements

Published material
Chorley, W.R. *Royal Air Force Bomber Command Losses of the Second World War 1943* (Midland Counties Publications, 1996)
Chorley, W.R. *Royal Air Force Bomber Command Losses of the Second World War 1945* (Midland Counties Publications, 1998)
Chorley, W.R. *Royal Air Force Bomber Command Losses of the Second World War Operational Training Units* (Midland Counties Publications, 2002)
Chorley, W.R. *To See the Dawn Breaking – 76 Squadron Operations* (Midland Counties Publications, 1981)
Everitt, C. and Middlebrook, M. *The Bomber Command War Diaries* (Midland Publishing Ltd, 1996)
Maitland, Andrew. *Through the Bombsight* (William Kimber, 1986)

Sources
No. 76 Squadron Operations Record Book, The National Archives, AIR 27 651
No. 608 Squadron Operations Book, The National Archives, AIR 27 2101
No. 1409 Flight Air Ministry Bulletin courtesy of Marcus Bicknell, whose late father Wing Commander Nigel Bicknell, DSO, DFC and bar, served with No. 1409 Flight, *https://marcusbicknell.wordpress.com/*
The U-boat wars 1939–1945 (Kriegsmarine) and 1914–1918 (Kaiserliche Marine) and Allied Warships of WWII, *https://www.uboat.net/*

Acknowledgements
Steve Darlow would like to thank Caroline Bolton, for access to Ferris Newton's memoir and further details of his life. Thanks also extend to Marcus Bicknell, Daniel Whatmough, Robin Brooks, Cherry Greveson, Squadron Leader Mark Discombe and Diane Law-Crookes. And to everyone at air shows and book-signing events who prompted George to tell his story; we may have used subterfuge, but we got there.

Index